Vanishing Points
NEW MODERNIST POEMS

ROD MENGHAM is Reader in Modern English Literature at Cambridge, where he is also Curator of Works of Art at Jesus College. He is the author of books on Charles Dickens, Emily Brontë and Henry Green, as well as of *The Descent of Language* (1993). He has edited collections of essays on contemporary fiction, violence and avant-garde art, and the fiction of the 1940s. He has written on art for various magazines and composes the catalogues for the biennial 'Sculpture in the Close' exhibition, at Jesus College, Cambridge. He is also the editor of the Equipage series of poetry pamphlets; his own poems have been published under the title *Unsung: New and Selected Poems* (Folio/Salt, 1996; 2nd edition 2001).

JOHN KINSELLA is the author of over twenty books, including *The Hunt* (Bloodaxe/FACP, 1998), *The Hierarchy of Sheep* (Bloodaxe/FACP, 2000/2001), *Auto* (Salt, 2000) and *Peripheral Light: Selected and New Poems* (W. W. Norton, 2003). He is editor of the international literary journal *Salt*, consultant editor of *Westerly*, Cambridge correspondent for *Overland*, and international editor of the American journal *The Kenyon Review*. He is a Fellow of Churchill College, Cambridge University, Adjunct Professor to Edith Cowan University and Professor of English at Kenyon College.

Vanishing Points

NEW MODERNIST POEMS

Edited by

ROD MENGHAM & JOHN KINSELLA

SALT

CAMBRIDGE

PUBLISHED BY SALT PUBLISHING
PO Box 937, Great Wilbraham, Cambridge PDO CB1 5JX United Kingdom
PO Box 202, Applecross, Western Australia 6153

This anthology © Rod Mengham and John Kinsella, 2004

First published 2004

Printed and bound in the United Kingdom by Lightning Source

Typeset in Swift 9.5 / 13

ISBN 1 876857 13 7 paperback

SP

1 3 5 7 9 8 6 4 2

Contents

Vanishing Points

PREFACE

It could be argued that the lyric in poetry is a *fait accompli*, that it is generic across languages and cultures. If musicality and the register of song inform the line of poetry, or are worked against, then the lyric becomes a truism. But the lyric is more than that. It's a political registration as well, a declaration of relationship between self and text, self and the empirical "outside". It declares an intentionality in appearance, in its desire for continuation.

Typically, a poem gives the reader or listener something to take away from the text—an emotional gravitas, whimsical joy, intellectual or spiritual connection or awakening. These expectations have been challenged and undermined overtly through the stages of Modernism, but such challenges are the proto-typical concern of the poet regardless of age or context: that is, the relationship between the originating words and word strings, and their intended audience. The ceremonial chant, the private utterance scribbled on a prison wall, the paternalisms of a society's laureate: it's a question of where the packages of word, or words, disseminate, take on lives of their own through the context of each individual or group encounter with the moment of utterance.

In a sense, the lyric is lost in the moment of realisation: it is that engagement with "self" and articulation, the many possible engagements of the lyrical "I" with signifier and signified. Modernism in poetry maps this frustration of self-expression. The ownership of certainty of observation—that what the poet sees and conveys to those other than him or herself is a constant—has been placed under pressure and found wanting. Social and cultural upheaval on an unprecedented scale, the destruction of natural "resources" (the word itself is a large part of the problem), and death by mechanisation have led to obvious shifts in notions of what constitutes the "I", or rather, what the "I" can validly express outside its own constructed empiricisms. This is, of course, a "culturo-centric" observation.

Context does matter. Someone writing a poem in a luxury apartment in a great city at the centre of a military empire does create a different intentionality from the singer composing with community members, expressing the group's marginalisation, loss, and defiance. The expression "avant-garde" is military in origin, be it from Napoleon's shock troops or dredged out of Mallory. The modernist avant-garde, and the avant-gardes that have emerged out of modernities, have worked to challenge a status quo, or to assert their differences in perception. A more just way of expressing, or expression comes into play. It's to do with "seeing", and conveying the politics of that seeing. The relationship between the poet and the tools of expression, and the tensions between experience and expression, are highlighted. Language is of the user, but the user is also a product of language. This paradox informs the desire to make of poetry a weapon to challenge a "false" or "deceptive" status quo. Be it the Dadaists after the First World War, or the play-ploys of Gertrude Stein, or the post-Vietnam War and Watergate eruption of Language poetry, or the smouldering rejectionism of the "Cambridge School", or the guerrilla de-hybridisations of Murri poet Lionel Fogarty. There is iconoclastic intent in each expression, and language is the weapon.

It could be argued, however, that the lyric has always been the vehicle for such expression, and the "form" itself—in its paradoxical combination of the universal and the centring of self—evolved as the most effective linguistic-musical vehicle for such expression of opposition. This anthology is an example of how diverse not only conceptualisations of the lyric are, but how malleable its co-ordinates can become. Each poet here is conscious of the implications of a text that might imprint itself on memory, the effects of the mnemonic, and the lyric's power of subliminal expression. Rather than see aggressive intentionality, one might equally see a responsibility and concern about the effect the lyric has once it leaves the space of composition. That words "change", that meaning alters according to context, are variable factors that ironically liberate rather than restrain the poem.

In the 1980s it was not unusual within European-language poetry communities to talk of the death of the lyric—especially within linguistically innovative circles of English-language poets. Maybe what was observed, or intended, was a rejection of the exclusiveness of the self, that the poem could exist in a bubble, "ignorant" of political responsibility. Of course, poetry was never so easy, whatever form it took, but the need to express such concerns—and to test these concerns within the structure of the poem itself—was strongly felt. In recent years, there's been talk of new lyricism, post-lyricism, and the gamut of groupings that comes with a need to reconcile past with present poeticising. There has been a sense of the meta-textual, but this is not necessarily a new thing. Thomas Stanley, "Lesser Caroline" poet, was a great translator. Most of his own compositions still show traces of those poets he translated. He brought Italian, French, and Greek conventions to play within his strictly formal English verse. He replayed popular conceits in new frameworks. He was an intellect; he was a meta-textual poet. The contemporary English-language innovative lyric captures some of this—text and sound to be received on a mnemonic level, but also need to be processed and thought about. Reading and listening should be work as well as reception.

Each of the poets in this anthology challenges us to think about how the lyric works, and whether it is a relevant literary concept in whatever environment/spatiality we experience it in. The power of the word itself, of the line, of the packaging and distribution of those lines, is in play. The lyric has never been the prisoner of convention that some would have us think—metrical consistency in English, or the conventions of the French syllabics (for example, with the alexandrine, placement of caesura, alternating rhymes, and so on) have always been displaced or eroded without the loss of lyrical effect. The metrically variable lyrics of Sidney through to the resonant paratac-tics of Prynne, have in no way impaired the singing of the language. Rather, they have developed sophisticated layerings of political possibility.

This is not a "school" of poets, but a grouping of unique voices. Some speak more directly to us than others, but the sheer power of the lyrical template must bring our certainties into question.

JOHN KINSELLA

INTRODUCTION

The vanishing point lies beyond the horizon established by ruling conventions, it is where the imagination takes over from the understanding. Most anthologies of contemporary verse are filled with poems that do not cross that dividing-line, but our contention is that many poems in this volume are situated on the threshold of conventional sense-making. They go beyond the perspective of accepted canons of taste and judgement and ask questions about where they belong, and who they are meant for, often combining the pathos of estrangement with the irascibility of the refusenik.

Stephen Rodefer's poem 'Brief to Butterick' (included here) encapsulates the position; it is simultaneously an elegy for a dead friend, a lament for the neglect of his poetry, and a diatribe against the editors of the Norton anthology who have excluded Oppen, Riding (and Butterick) from their selection. Rodefer's poem is a kind of counter-anthology, since it quotes several lines by Butterick and places them alongside allusions to Auden and Shakespeare. This editorial activity, which relates both the subject and the poet himself to a tradition of writing and to certain principles of recognition, memorialises both of them far more effectively than the offer of walk-on parts in the Norton anthology could ever have done.

All anthologies enter the world fully aware of their genealogy, of where they fit in, of how they relate to certain traditions of writing by affiliation or rejection. This combination of dependent and independent gestures is inevitable, particularly in the case of selections of work aligned with national or regional versions of literary history. The present anthology does not fall into that category; its international reach does not, however, bring exemption from the dilemma of wanting to stand apart from conditions of rivalry while also needing to claim a special value in comparison with publications already available.

The means by which an international anthology might take up its position are simultaneously more elusive in one way and more decisive in another. Insofar as its relationship to national traditions of practice and debate has been relaxed, to the same degree the requirement to identify alternative criteria of selection and association is more insistent. Our subtitle proposes elements of continuity with an historically identifiable form of international writing that sets at a premium experiments with form and language. One thing our selection does is to reflect the extent to which the community of experimental poets is now, at the beginning of the twenty first century, genuinely international in its scope and in the directness of its interactions. Since the mid-1960s, the poetic avant-gardes of several English language-speaking countries have depended on communication with like-minded groups in other countries far more than with the mainstream writers they are geographically lumped together with. The writers in this anthology have been part of a process of exchanging ideas manifested in little magazines, in the publishing programmes of small presses, and in the sheer volume of email and internet transactions. Contemporary innovative poetry of the kind selected here is genuinely and profoundly international in character.

Most (arguably all) of the writers in this volume represent a strand in recent poetry that has stayed in touch with the agendas of modernism; they are not postmodernist, but late modernist writers. Each writer has a definable project, her or his work refers to a body of concepts even if the literary method employed appears to be non-referential; each has maintained a significant degree of contact with the speaking voice, even when the manner in which the speaking voice has dominated the history of literature in English is challenged and complicated; all are concerned with working in or against the grain of the literary forms and genres that have evolved in the course of that same history.

This is not an anthology of 'language' writing. The roster of names includes senior figures whose careers began prior to the launch of 'Language' magazine and its attendant, postmodernist ideology. It also includes the names of poets associated with 'Language' whose work has developed in quite independent directions over the last two decades; and the range of styles represented here includes the work of younger writers who regard their poetry as subsequent and alternative to the example set by 'Language'. What binds together their various kinds of innovative practice is a strong insistence on finding ways of continuing and renewing the lyric impulse in poetry in English. What is equally important is a commitment to work that examines the political scope of poetry, that questions the grounds of spokesmanship in a world that is simultaneously global and local, that takes seriously, has ambitions for, the social responsibility of poetry and its relationship to other, culturally powerful discourses; poetry that critiques, and is unashamedly antithetical to, the discourses of power.

All anthologists stake out their territory by an appeal to large intellectual and cultural ambitions realized though the agency of a medium that often seems untranslatable into such terms. The big, sweeping claims can be seriously embarrassed by the resort to individual poems whose main purpose is to work with language in ways that are incommensurate with other forms of knowledge. We risk the claims, nevertheless, trusting our judgements about a body of work that brings together a diversity of ways in which poetry constitutes itself as antagonism, as the ideally situated forum for confrontations between public and private meaning, between individual rights and ideas of the common good, between song and jargon, testimony and cliché, the somatic and the civic. The vanishing point is where these tensions are poised, creatively unresolved, somewhere off the map of conventional half-measures that so many anthologies have inured us to.

Rod Mengham

1 JOHN ASHBERY

All Messages Have Been Played

A chance encounter—he'd
dropped a stitch somewhere along the way
to a palimpsest. Put it all there
and then wonder why it was done?

You don't need to die there.
A freshet is ever restless,
the stars coming undone in a way
thought to be magic before there was magic,

dim process of stars.
It seems to have gone back
to doing what it was doing all along.
Maybe we'll enjoy these together.

There were more of us
then, when we seemed so few.
This plenteous space confined us—
an afternoon of succulents, hens and chicks,

the rusted roadster. The waterfall *is* the window.
You can see through it. Still more of us.
Have her meet you at the party for the residents.
But the poetry—how do you handle it?

A Holding Mode

Out of a pure blue sky, on East River dusk,
memories of misbehavior soldier on,
still fresh in their minds.

Because the night didn't favor it
I did advise these to leave me.
Nothing more was said for several months.
Then, like a bee one has to swat,
it was August again.

Just so far could he go.
She didn't seem to defer to his
idea of tacit cooperation.
It was a compliment or a complement.

The huge pallor is shouldered
like an opera cape; gloves are clasped
in an incidentally waiting hand.
Should we stay? Would there,
in any case, be time to see more,
see further? When the government orders
every fourth bayonet seized, do we strip naked,
or is a holding mode indicated?

Franchises in Flux

Another chambered nautilus bequeathed me
this other portent, the new present,
and I am glad now,
fuzzy, even.

That you got off at your stop
makes it correct. As for my behavior,
who knows? Tangoing in from thither
Texas, could you add a name to the scroll?

We foregathered in the scrub forest on the bluff
the loudspeakers reached. "And who is to say
who says it? You must promise to leave your regrets
among the chaff and shucks. That way,
they'll never haunt you."

Back in the city square it seems as though
the quiet had never been dispersed.
Panhandlers and cheerleaders pass as in a daze.
Only hitchhikers seem alert

to the favors God distributes to His guests.
Some, if not all, are sleeping,
planning to make amends when they waken
at a time convenient to both parties.

If you hadn't liked these, why
take them away to Tartarus, where approving
moms will never see them, dab
at a tear with folded hanky?

And on the tenth step, turn and pretend to waver.
Pigeons are alive and wheeling. It's not spring,
it's winter, but tropical clouds damp
down the horizon. In the spirit of lifting, march.

Nut Castle

Somehow the intentness of the whole
moment of watching takes hold
and is obsolete.

A sneering star lit up the casual
abstracted look of the place.

There's no dodging the confederacy once it consents
to call itself that.
Until then there's the turbulent exit to write about
and—yes—perhaps think:

oiled portraits backing up for miles,
a meadow, past its prime and still virgin.

Interesting People of Newfoundland

Newfoundland is, or was, full of interesting people.
Like Larry, who would make a fool of himself on street corners
for a nickel. There was the Russian who called himself
the Grand Duke, and who was said to be a real duke from somewhere,
and the woman who frequently accompanied him on his rounds.
Doc Hanks, the sawbones, was a real good surgeon
when he wasn't completely drunk, which was most of the time.
When only half drunk he could perform decent cranial surgery.
There was the blind man who never said anything
but produced spectral sounds on a musical saw.

There was Walsh's, with its fancy grocery department.
What a treat when Mother or Father
would take us down there, skidding over slippery snow
and ice, to be rewarded with a rare fig from somewhere.
They had teas from every country you could imagine
and hard little cakes from Scotland, rare sherries
and Madeiras to reward the aunts and uncles who came dancing.
On summer evenings in the eternal light it was a joy
just to be there and think. We took long rides
into the countryside, but were always stopped by some bog or other.
Then it was time to return home, which was OK with everybody,
each of them having discovered he or she could use a little shuteye.

In short there was a higher per capita percentage of interesting people
there than almost anywhere on earth, but the population was small,
which meant not too many interesting people. But for all that
we loved each other and had interesting times
picking each other's brain and drying nets on the wooden docks.
Always some more of us would come along. It is in the place
in the world in complete beauty, as none can gainsay,
I declare, and strong frontiers to collide with.
Worship of the chthonic powers may well happen there
but is seldom in evidence. We loved that too,
as we were a part of all that happened there, the evil and the good

and all the shades in between, happy to pipe up at roll call
or compete in the spelling bees. It was too much of a good thing
but at least it's over now. They are making a pageant out of it,
one of them told me. It's coming to a theater near you.

Meaningful Love

What the bad news was
became apparent too late
for us to do anything good about it.

I was offered no urgent dreaming,
didn't need a name or anything.
Everything was taken care of.

In the medium-size city of my awareness
voles are building colossi.
The blue room is over there.

He put out no feelers.
The day was all as one to him.
Some days he never leaves his room
and those are the best days,
by far.

There were morose gardens farther down the slope,
anthills that looked like they belonged there.
The sausages were undercooked,
the wine too cold, the bread molten.
Who said to bring sweaters?
The climate's not that dependable.

The Atlantic crawled slowly to the left
pinning a message on the unbound golden hair of sleeping
        maidens,
a ruse for next time,
where fire and water are rampant in the streets,
the gate closed—no visitors today
or any evident heartbeat.

I got rid of the book of fairy tales,
pawned my old car, bought a ticket to the funhouse,
found myself back here at six o'clock,
pondering "possible side effects."

There was no harm in loving then,
no certain good either. But love was loving servants
or bosses. No straight road issuing from it.
Leaves around the door are pencilled losses.
Twenty years to fix it.
Asters bloom one way or another.

Wolf Ridge

Attention, shoppers. From within the inverted
commas of a strambotto, seditious whispering
watermarks this time of day. Time to get out
and, as they say, about. Becalmed on a sea
of inner stress, sheltered from cold northern breezes,
idly we groove: Must have
been the time before this, when we all moved
in schools, a finny tribe, and this way
and that the caucus raised its din:
punctuation and quips, an "environment"
like a lovely shed. My own plastic sturgeon
warned me away from knowing. Now look at the damage.
You can't. It's invisible. Anyway, you spent his love,
swallowed everything with his knives,
a necessary unpleasantness viewed from the rumble seat
of what was roaring ahead.

I want to change all that.
We came here with a mandate of sorts, anyway
a clear conscience. Attrition and court costs
brought you last year's ten best. Now it's firm
and not a bit transparent. Everybody got lost
playing hide and seek, except you,
who were alone. Not a bad way to end the evening,
whistling. They wanted a bad dinner,
and at this time a bad dinner was late.
Meatloaf, you remembered, is the third vegetable.

The Template

was always there, its existence seldom
questioned or suspected. The poets of the future
would avoid it, as we had. An imaginary railing
disappeared into the forest. It was here that the old gang
used to gather and swap stories. It
was like the Amazon, but on a much smaller scale.

Afterwards, when some of us swept out into the world
and could make comparisons, the fuss seemed justified.
No two poets ever agreed on anything, and that amused us.
It seemed good, the clogged darkness that came every day.

Hungry Form

1.

Starting with a projectile
careless half-blind
raging
distracted
a magnified attention
to keep us all transfixed

the want that will the mind is fat and smooth
the forest out of which I grow
no rest nor peace the repossessed
this hungry form this
form to form

a bleeding mouth
that speaks for all
when speaks for none
but one as one
not-two

wants by sucking dry
travels light but leaves
excessive trails
contained yet open
not-split but reproducible
senses no motion
but its own

divest all knowledge
as its own
"bear me
all names tell my story"

upon which lifting
upon whose task a great many heads
I ask for records
I clamour for speech
what's mine to carry

2.

Coming up to the time of shock
of addition of surplus
we're standing
to be counted
official numbering invariably fails
by tens of by hundreds of
thousands
the feast is hidden and the promise unclear

could I of all
a time like this
but for
a time like this!

manicured
combed to a lilt
long derided
physically paled
shamed by rumoured
approximation
female to bone
woman to a knee
not by half yet halved
find myself clasped

by the red-hot coreless core of this
Your ever-opening genitalia!

fear amasses along the borders
whispers the one always throws

the second stone
hides the first
unleashes many

3.

Let be possessed
what is in-truth
I say
another splits
into small specks
at heart of day
at hottest spot

sizzling bushes
are barricades
burning streets sweat out pictures
and pictures of pictures
and pictures of pictures of pictures

You forced your arm in
so deeply carved yet another set of I forced
my arm in so deeply carved yet another set of
lips legs legacies
"unlearn, unlearn"
whispers the one who
slowly I slide
further into shadow
my insatiable body haunt
"never would
assimilate pleasure with the death!"

death takes to pleasure like a ghost
I rise for the future
I rise for the past
can hardly come
Enough today
can hardly form
Enough to care
this recklessly

    4.

Wouldn't I say
untimeliness
lack of collective sense
make such an event
in-fact abridgeable

while I (another)
rush for corder
with which to angle
the incredible stuff
pours out an alarming riot
ah-ah always
stand for this

bloated
disproportionate sense
of reality
spreading form
affects all form
cooling half-selves half cover-up

"just as it is
being released into synthetic space"
makes out
an added count

nightlines are crisp
with cellular apparitions

   5.

Pocketing rage
carefully
as if in-truth motionless
unattached
empty form
most absorbing
being most detached
maculate untwinned
wonderfully penetrable

"release me from socket"
I cry turning the corner
"treacherous lyric
mystic bind of encasement"
"give me a break give me heart
not a couple of guitars"
shrugs another looks away

in-meat trick for trick
truth for truth

   6.

All the while
conjugation

all things coupled into shape
pathologically two
is in one
for the love of
my-country

two is one
true fever
not one to one
nor two is two
two is for one
true peace

just as it is
so it will be
made to the count

"being
not-one nor here
does half unpromised not
make me
as two is theirs
as one is by half
thus halved is more full
than one empty of two
yet one to two
(and three and four)
and femaled when I meet you"
I say pondering on the grammars of form

ah but one by one
and all to one
full to the one
empty that is full
emptied then empty

always more empty than full
(interrupts another)
in the logic of war
one disregarded
is not entertained

You pulled your arm your shoulder your head
out suddenly

the lick of fire your reds of deep are all a mass
another walks through
I'm just sick of the pain
doesn't stay for two

a one is a one
transport occurs
speak to stand
what kind of onion
our numbers are numerous
peels in-difference
what lifted shades
what looseness today
and sense of concordance

3 LEE ANN BROWN

My epithalamion

a bird sound at the end of every sentence
the period dissolves and becomes a curve of notes
from lake of souls (reading notes
— ROBIN BLASER

on the morning of my would be wedding
I wake up and turn again to poetry
halfway cross the continental drift
towards a blazing island
I open the Holy Forest
to middle epithalamion
and later tell Robin the story
of how maybe now
I am married to poetry
and he says But don't let *him* go
and I don't for a little bit longer
but now everything is changed and not
so bad as I bed down with poetry and myself
whom I each love entwined real love and would welcome
       another

You Are Not Gorgeous and I Am Coming Anyway

You are gorgeous and I am not getting to know you any better I feel
Broken into I feel drench dreamed
With the Woolworth's worth of dimestore socks
Photographed and networked up a racoon's nest

Not here in the city but in the ill de la cité
Hungry for some foreign country
In the middle of my jury duty crawl into bed exhumed from Bjork's
  Champagne toast
To all of Iceland's fairy cultures recorded as the doors swing open and
  shut

Of course you are gorgeous and I & I am coming
It happens every day and then I fall into the crick again
Spattered with immediate boredom
Feeding two boys not one and neither of them hitting home

Transposed to trappist ringers, Nick called this morning from Assisi,
Last words as the phone card ran out blinking from 600 lire down

See you in the next life

My Uncruel April, My Totally Equal Unforetold April Unfolded

Added cups and plates
            rotate other stars
                      in your sequential platforms.

As with all good (real) poetry movements we splice the past
Aprils, walking near himself before there, her pleated heart,
        heated.

The Question Undoes Itself on an organic twittering machine
Trumpet vine of the Bottle Brush Fire
Escape playing itself on the grassy beds

Of Hyancinth, light-bulbed, headboarded, made up,
Observed, vibratory-color bannered sheets of
Fire Sabi beauty, old peeling, jumbled, a mess.

The purple Third Avenue L, the Horrors of Spring.

Ecstatically crying, to peaceful well-being
Maintenance of the handful of unhatched speckled
Eggs thrown from the next nest, mixed with
The hand-drawn line so far from your usual practice.

The Impulse to Call & Spring Upon

As incremental desire is counted out
So I kiss closer and closely to your mouth
The No Blame Chaos Form complete

A surge protects our hearts from sleep
To see you closely, across from me, I'm
rising, decisive, almost shy

Your eyes, lionine—my poetry
Risks gushing kisses so I close my song,
Anticipating our playing long

              I didn't know how
this little
              song would
end
the last stanza not right
until last night
       when
to change the form
to Leonine
everything
             like the form
      is changed

a long long line
      like your sweet kisses
which liquefy
my limbs
      & get better & better
                impossibly
                  real

Respond to me

Respond to me: how many
iniquities have I and fish. Scholar me
& delicate easterns to me.

Simple curs abscond with you
& are arbitrarily inimicable to you?

Against leaves, what raptors I buy

East and potentates to aim
and stipendly sic'um on persecutors:

Writers & enemies against my sailor lovers
consume me, consume my fish
my many sad scents

Positronic in my nervous pedestals
& observing all vastness
my many cementings
& my vestigial feet meow considerately:

How quasi I redo considerable sums, how
invested, how comedic a tin ear.

shiny jewel eye

with Julie Patton, Euphrosyne Bloom & Meg Arthurs in mind

These flower forms vary to me in ways I can't say yet but you know
already before me in your dress lace—no "A" on the off white
(cream) lady bugged familiar to the wall pointing to Big Ohio
Egyptian football in & out motion of your arms passion freak—out
on our own time—to the triumphs flower—the stole slipped, the
slip stole—no limits on the feintly fealty couch—passive as he was
—(I'm huge)—the hinge bing-cherried out & tweaked on the
Byronic road ironic—drownded in the lake of Prague's Guarda—
Valve without me—he's—free—and Sphinx-like as I write the night
again so quic—The Dion Ferry is X-otic—water taxied over
Manhatta's spires

where (back in time) she was living in Alphabet City with all the
little stories she never tells:

While throwing an apple peel over her shoulder she suddenly real-
izes she's been living in Description City all along. A big, blue
letter "A" is motioning for her over to take off her veil and play, but
she says 'fuck that' while chewing on her candy cigarette. The
Phantom Tollbooths, otherwise known as the Fuss Puppets, are
now warming up in the next room covered entirely with writing.
One says "Dogmatic No Radio" and another, just "Spike."
    Ms. (Blank) was trying to think but it was real hard because of
all the buzzing. People kept trying to get her attention and succeed-
ing. She had started to live alone once, but like honey he started
living there too, postponing her growing up for a few more
months.
    She lived in the zone whose even years no solstice interrupt. A
certain surgeon had a beautiful garden there. He stuttered even
further when trying to speak his own name. There remains a small
scar on her forefinger where she cut herself badly in the university
kitchens. Blood ran all down her apron as she inadvertently carried
the large carrot, repairing back to her room. A Russian Formalist
toy made of colored wood was sitting there.

She then converted to Sarah Beattyism and then more slowly to Quietism. *Single Girl, Single Girl, Goes where she please. Married Girl, Married Girl: Baby on her knees. Baby on her knees.* If one more guy tells me they like that song, I'm going to *Crown* Him (in not a nice way).

Hot nights in the summer bedroom astrological Grand Central Station. Fox Point Kitchen Dance. Mingus was a Big Band trying to affect my body with some immediate gravity. Sex do to me one's catalogue and while you're at it Rimbaud. The cats had better but fewer houses. Let all mortal flesh keep silent over that one. The seraphim with ceaseless eye knew his metempsychosis was incomplete.

So formally, she was nowhere yet. But the dream takes its own form, organically arranged like a bento box, that is, organic within the waking grid.

A Call for Vertical Integration in the Eye of the Storm

Purple & blue Tiffany combo in the
Church of my childhood struggle of perfect
Public meat longing again vine-covered
Power flower conflict hunger for green

Struggle—if this is sin then separation—
Grace abounds even more than bonds—
Doubt boundaries not programmable—
Stretched grace strikes us down—
Social eels demand ransom, children

Do not bow your heads—tranquility of hymns
Is shattered & addressed two days ago I
Saw the Black Ash of a Church Burned on its
Sure Foundation   Century old pin oaks scorched

Against stones of those who can't ever leave this sight—
Who witnessed   Who
Drove away during the sermon   Burning

---

*Note by way of Explanation
from the*

Double Southern Register
or is it

The Southern Lyre?

Who is burning these churches? Make them stop!
After weaving our way through the new upscale Charlotte city-limit subur-
ban scrawl out Rae Road through her country memory, my mom and I
persuade the cop protecting the vacated scene to let us past the yellow and
black plastic ribbons to see the smoldered mess, not much left—blackened
beams, jambs kicked in by anonymous torch, red clay wet from last night's
useless hoses—a little house with vacant front porch right across the street—
I imagine the fear and go home and write this poem.
    In *The Mind of the South*, W.J. Cash wrote that he and his generation "hated
(the South) with the exasperated hate of a lover who cannot persuade the
object of his affections to his desire."

Charlotte,

I love you deeply.

That's why I had to leave.

I see your changes keyed up rapidly flashing past the new contra dance named the Independence Boulevard which is way convoluted like the traffic which is nothing compared to here, up North from whence I sign this letter,

Letter Out, Letter Back

Encyclopedia Botanica

or

A Mother-to-Be's Book of meltdown anticipation and scientific renderings of organic and theoretical forms such as the way flowers lie in the bud: A permutational Cento of Centos consisting of painful insufflations, multiple estivations, the calculus of various inflorescents, my naive set theories (unordered pairs), vibratory odes in all manner of cross-pollinating color, illumined spores & how they grow in corkscrew contortion, all imbued with entire New Electric Libraries of the Body. Herein find random factors of the strange attraction to "hard science," but also to soften it, previously FAILED materials and pick-up works, illuminated maps of misreading, specifically, a Trace Study of my Own Peculiar Vocabulary living in the dictionary, reading public signs backwards or torqued in the House (See: "Waking in the Offices of Dawn," "A Demand for Fried Chicken," and "The Hinged Bride's Index Box"). A deep pillow tapestry, the soft underbelly of the (not guilty) quilt-lined snow on 100's of 1000's of flowers packed in wet newspaper to last this linked act always with an Other in mind: molecules being excited to a higher level of activity by heat or unseen stimulations, through any reader's eye to correspondence's finger, culminating in a Splice Index for the edification of Ladies, Gentlemen, Sentences & new Punkish Geezers left out in the rain of the sleep cake that changed Everything.

If Emily would be a little more Whitmanic she'd be me.

A Cut Velvet Version

Full Spectrum Song Cycle
A Cento Cycle of Desire
These Cento Songs are Wet Airs on
Tweaked Vellum
Sustaining the Vibration

4   BRIAN CATLING

The Pittancer

1

Sparrows dry hearts
fluttered in Joseph's tree
as the city approaches day by day
on cracked and creaking souls.
Even the snow lost,
amid the hill's rise
& fall
dawn
leatherish
disgust.

He carried
the gummy stick
and blood to the snowline
between wolves and haunted fellows
whose simple reverence weeped all the way
home &
dusk
magnified
holiest ground.

2

From out the mouth
cuts saw a bitter gall,
 ink hidden in boiled and drained angel's sleeves.
Sitting in that now most unlikely tree.

The Rye ghost
Love & Hate
tattooed on either hand.
Hands matured with the wood,
polished to talon more than bless.

It is a suit
dummy fastened
tourist to a scarecrow's sight,
 propped to clue the quarried vision's tilt.
Fake as the poet's stone, name carved in absences
of the bodies scent. The true intelligence is
graced elsewhere.

3

The tree itself has shuddered out,
inverting its gesture in vaulting mirrors
beneath the pitched soil.
The roots describing the exact branches
of that day, the very twigs configured to the moment
that he saw, woven between the wind and rain a smile
in the trembling leaves.

Today the needles and dog shit
have calligraphed a signature,
on the spot, over the stump sealed
by a scarring of indifference:
times insolent lime.
The roots have twitched
 sucking night down to beckon
& wave in another light,
compressed by the darker groaning loam,
 squeezed into sound and the raking opposites of shadows
that flatter the illuminations of worms,
 in this little land of hearing.

4

This is where the angel dwells.
integral with the intimate earth,
sheltering like the dead for a while,
 buffeted by moles, stitched by ants
and embroidered by dim fungi's care.
This is where it with its retinue of phosphor
waits,
& avoids the sullen evolution of Satan's mechanical gates,
 ingeniously turning sight to loutish gum.
Voicing the moment to abrade the hour,
spiting old lies like seeds to fulminate and cull
the rind of earth made shallow, dogmatic
as a plate of sand.

5

Those that prowl
the tangled edge of
the prophet's garden song, do so, in silence.
else they become dubbed or scolded,
accused of maim or terror at the chewed contours of speech,
gummed wet and serrated blue.
Animals, listening with great ugliness to the sound of the meat-
      breath word;
CHILD
and dribble a padded track in circles around this screen,
the dusk is cocked in a sallow bulb,
 your attention, lured,
letting the wilderness run tight between
burnt sand strangled to glass, counting
grain by grain,
the face turning to stone,
chiselled to stillness the mouth and the camera's heat
in advance of the wind, mad with oil smoke & genies.

6

This is where the man-beast crawls
the angel turned inside out, made raw,
growing vines and sinews backwards through the flesh,
guilt gnawing the nails into claws
prophet hair, soured to dreadlocks itch
inside the haggard wining heart.

last seen at Passiondale
performing schism
in planetary blood
so that no water-colour youth will
ever nimbly step
again from painted sun to
crescent silvered moon.

The artist also saw the island
hewn, its ragged splintered spine
flung past history in a sticky arc.
An obedience wand, thrown to be chased
way outside the domain of trust, in a curdling place
grown old.

7

A penny weight
of blood, worth
a tint of myrrh or
less on the wren scale.

> Its pixie heart
> hooked
> thorn to thorn
> a nutmeg of
> clockwork
> in the damp
> shock of branches.

A blot of tear
in a decade of vellum,
rolled; telescoping
the salt pellet road
weighed against
the stair of evaporated
sanity
&
the star of
impenetrable sight.

8

He walks down
the sliding snowfields
into that village
smoking amber with song
anvils & preparation.

A pagan Christ
has stepped beside
 him on the loud
narrow frost track,
                    collecting blind
                    wishes after dawn.
Crows & bells
Have spoken
Over them
& nagged at their
plumes of breath.

9

Inside a sleeve of rain
Snot knotted at the wrist
Joint,
Linked silver in a quisling gesture,
curt anticipation nudges the credence table
Shaking the earthbound chandelier of teeth
Now
our pilgrim's wine
won't be tested thus.

        Embarrassment
        Gathers and evicts us;
        bleak brown shadows, smaller than mice.

later,
the slithered cosy pelt
of our ventriloquist's memory
will unfreeze,
sniffing like a fuse at the succession of birth,
warm and constant, spoken into the long track
of transmutation so that we might sleep
between the possessions,
affirmed.

10

But now
in a show
of pages, painted
& scrolled
in cuckooed a
photo.

Lambeth
Eighty years later,
But before he world changed.

The scull of the docks is very
black & white allsocket water,
boat jaws and empty lipped
windows spitting distance
from his house
and garden,
fit & ruffled out
of class.

The river is busy
and peopleless,
stuck.
A pause
in a puppet show
changing hands,
and hot faced gloves
under the stage
in advance of
plight.

5 DAVID CHALONER

Waste

how many ciphers
scratch the surface
of digital complexity
or fathom choreography's
sleek shift
determined moves
and yes
the particular
as a shade of mind
oblivious to the obvious curiosities
inherent in such abundance
such determination
stunning light
and gratuitous acts of clarity
negotiation and cynicism
dream this at your peril
spit jets of fervent ideology
across the promised connection
to locate
grounded but able
to propose the impossible
pull me from the margin
boat of language
cruising your reference
to transfer a whereabouts
receding as distance
rejects inclusion

Unnamed

in the ankle
not only the Achilles
but a tender spot
frail seed bed

mightier ways than
intercontinental transfer
zipped in time zone fabric

pressure your being invokes
westerly storm fronts
nineteen degrees centigrade
wafer sun setting
through pollution's mask

blight on wilderness
hot springs urgency
provoking ease

missiles have been
turned away from
the island
south china news
assures

this effort seems bleak
by comparison

the place we're in
a pianist sits each afternoon
confronting the indifference
with harmonic narrative
consumed by desire
an inexorable change
a fortune cookie insists
my troubles will soon

be over
but not to a tune by
Rogers and Hammerstein

oh no
more like freedom
experienced by the ultimate
global sparrow
pecking in the dust
of pre-storm geometry

Emblem

your look to me
is shadow lost
in pastoral danger

both shade and light
succumb to pious nature

an equation set to stun
the oracle of earthly flesh
constructed from eternity's waste
a place to worship
questioning and pain

struck dumb
await the formal gesture
of result
acquisition and conflict

never to
more simply answer
dark divide by colour
and illuminance

cough discretely against a code
of generous bluff
nowhere so unfathomable
as triangulated construct
faultlessly defined
pure register averts catastrophe
unveiled belatedly
at another place

the oils of ancient ceremony
drip from opened palms
fire stitches curious seams
to the currency of response

Spring and Other Places

reduced to ash and collected cold from spent flame
taken snow-borne to extinction

name me white reliquary as the snow makes flurry
overtly stated the complexity of farewell
renders salutation apt
in necessary simplicity prone to comfortable exaggeration
put in silence as the many rooms continue at their gathering

broken field
tracked by human, animal and apparatus, still though
and final, pushed to edge the crumbling cloud gone feint

coarse weed and moss shaped by the ungloved hand
to trace a shroud of harmony and delusion
air placing speechless measures at rest between us

distance not visible in light
calculations modified by the heart at rest
confusions of purpose and determined intent
meet this sentence
in its exquisite silence, a place without shadows
a name losing its echo

Thicket of Time

there are many beginnings
exchange of information
is constant
some are here
where we live
sometimes the sound of oral
transactions lasts for days
at night the lull is frightening
a breathless self-contained hush
of resistance a line deleted
by the glare of the inconsequential
the risk of breaking curfew
extreme although probable
this return
co-ordinates in a language of
darkness and ceremony
knives cross and separate
vivid shields
chemical pockets
rough privilege
you disengage
the smell of mould clings
unremarkably to our garments
someone enquires
a blue light equals desire
no one notices
there is no significance
to the encoding
we are contrite though we wish
otherwise
losing your head they say
imagine
years that last forever
her image fading
in Bergmanian angst
I am to ask about tradition

formality
divine influence
treachery of lines intersecting
in a neutralised skull
obsolete borders
governing vectors that deny
divine influence
tell me she says
about this exquisite crisis
once more repeat
most ordinary tones
dead promise
lost assurance
the forgotten reason
a mantle laden
green foliage
of violent acknowledgement
the green of chemical
outrage
the green of dials and digital
readout
the blip in the night sky
a dead planet projected
limitless hand of technology
filaments alive with the hum
of intelligent cross-referencing
systematic modal application
we live in a city
sometimes parts of us
wish otherwise
my glance faxes its intention
to a network
of possible receivers
words exhalations utterance
antique language of desire
the roads surrender
sonnets are tattooed across
your thighs

we meet
in the flickering ethereal light
of deserted control rooms
air seething static

Vista Vert

in spite of stillness
of wires
mist spins off
the blank gaze

illusions pass through
forenoon
the antiseptic that defines
extremes

drops
like a counterpane
ethereal mesmeric
diluting stale hours

pale and silent
by dawn the made bed
re-occupies
its vacancy

flying over the pasture's
nourishment
hour by hour
blue transparency

a sigh
that slides
against the faded wall
when sky devoid
of sense
donates still surface
to foreign shores
where a group

sits to eat and argue
casually
their presence
captivates a day perplexed

hour after hour
migrates
through north light
contradictory bright

curtains swerve
across the frame
the table
of events is set

trace boundaries
the idle attention
energy invisible
like certain colours

confront forms
claim their words
prove nothing
a complex need

light falls on darkness
translucent to clear
the balance reveals
an equal

in its wake

6 ANDREW CROZIER

Humiliation in its Disguises

Don't ask whose face it is when you see me
Being seen in search of your reflection

Scorched earth to the sky stopped with trees and clouds
Dumb reverie recoiled with sightless gaze
Our combat weaves through air and falls with us

Over the fluent nightfall of your rest
The costs of many bargains are exchanged
Moonlight like ice a frozen lake like sleep
Are copies made good as their replicas

The silences of portraits and dumb friends
Turn walls to margins corners sidle round
Start on arrival and shown poised to flee
Still the day lengthens colours mix and fade
A scarlet strip of empire in repose

Rooms contradict the curved weight of fatigue
Repeated details spectral and remote
Turn their straight lines from side to side and down
Where withered beauty turns its head and waits

This sacred place exposed to daily use
Shows by the flames by bare familiar trees
By recognition held back from a glance

Divisions interposed and lost in space
Darkness in layers stunned with eyes and tongues

Rise to the surface both dissolve and set

Blank Misgivings

Our father death speaks through the child our father
the sailor lost beside a dream of immense steppes
perfectly rigged violets inside a sunken bottle
tears condensed beneath the clear glass in the path

O fly you creatures, asiatic cranes and gazelles
slender ribbed of arctic birch and whalebone
air twists into grey sheets of old starlight
the extinct hiss of incendiary in a bombed cellar

This morning's trace of footprints leads back where
sidereal years modelled in spars and struts
thrust from the ground, stumps of brickwork
a broken corner where the sky turns cold

Remember such things under the new city
shadows of ruin swept into unlit night
one bare horizon drawn across another
day into day breaks the calamity of the heart

What to call to out of ignorance and loved best
the abrupt twilight and the unexpected dawn
when brief cries summon falls unanswering voice
pauses between the echoes of the century

Listen to the wagons thunder and the static roar
light outlined burning through the grid
the abandoned garden and the tumbled fence
alike and other unbuilt monuments to hope

The stones rest as they fall, the dying fall
among the dead and I could wish their bones
at rest their day so what there was each find
so be it the unhoped-for be no more than man

Andy-the-German Servant of Two Masters

The right family connections
and an edited biography. Deep cover
and a foreseen shortage of infantry wars. Theorist
of stalking. Long-range shooting
is mainly
a *spiritual* thing

The first thing you do, you get them
to buy automatic weapons
This breaks the ice and makes their fingers tingle.
One hand on the bottle and one . . .

Andy, Mr *Bundesverfassungsschutz* is not Budweiser,
Talked as much as someone with a mouthful of water.
That is, he swallowed the words and passed the water out as
        social gifts
How much can a building really take?

ritsch, ratsch
hang out the trash. The jury will buy
a limited hang-out. America for the Americans
Shine for the shoeshine boys
Land for the lords. Sacks for the shucks.
Elohim City for Oklahoma.
Draff for the hogs. Fish for the seals.
A bag for the sleaze. A bowl for the dust.

Time for crime. Day for night. Green for red.

Beyond the beaming tautologies, everything
profound loves a mask, and
people with dirty souls
don't wear swoop necklines.
The ATF guys weren't in the office that day
the office blew out of the building
Blew the town. No-showed their showdown.
Blow the gaff. Cut the smoke
in the open-plan with its façade cut away
to foreclose the government. Blow it out your ears.

Ozarks-scale gene pool bi-bi-bitten by a gun bug
Doorstep Andy selling a script
like throwing sticks for a dog.

Way down
way over where the steel rods breach
where the steel pins break-dance
where the parked cookup cracks the theorised linear frame,
watch out! where the classic curve of a blast wave
met the tectonic cement cubes
at the imaginary point in geometry;
and a citizen's rights man
with a doctorate in the mathematic of ruin,
brass Air Force general with
big back-up in negative civil engineering says
no way
could McVeigh have torn their playhouse down
We control the horizontal
He heard a skip-beat in the wall of sound

we control the vertical.
The updating of moral consensus. The conduct
of the gaze. Altering shared ideas
by cover of night. Sending to fantasies.
Threads run out as clues
adding grey noise to data excess
in a screen with key escrow. Where sight lines converge,

pinned against the horizon, a thief sideways
behind your back. How come the musicians know
what's coming next? From shoo-in to death-watch,
spinning data back through a false third party.
Hiding pattern in pattern, breaking outlines,
snap-point shear from appliquéd charges on the pillars.

I'm gonna run to the City of Refuge,
turn about, hire a captain of the watch
with the skills of a career infantry officer,
crossing the Great Plains without breaking a contour line.
The oculist of blind spots just walked in through the in door.
Fully automatics for the camp guards.
Elohim City Compound
is the outside of the inside.

Andy two for one. Andy fluent in the manly skills,
draw them in over the head handy.
The barrels are beautifully rifled and the marksmen
are destabilised, we figure
someone who believes what we believe
is too double dumb to double talk
a trick track where the phase of confined movement
flows on from conducted freedom of action.

Blow, Illinois, blow! the righteous highs
of homesteader holdouts, Indian killers
and Bible readers, stake racers
and redneck heads of household;
their gold,
            guns
                    and water
clinking on taut skin, tall-walkers
waving half a wit taught
civics by an
occupation government. Up-country
applejack and freeze-dried buffalo cocks.
Plenty too smart to eat soil.

Keepsakes from the Dolly Parton Theme Park,
Theologoumena in No Roads County.

A fervour of conjecture
where whatever fleshes out the fixed idea
is drawn in to draw on,
bent surface proteins as wrappers for
the end of the game. It was like selling
perimeter captains to paranoids.
While the verses give no light, living out of
the back of a truck, running with
a travelling gun fair, the country
flaring behind you like a contrail, from mesas
to trailer parks, wrapped up tight at
the vanishing point. the round jumps straight
and for a moment
your soul is held between your shoulder and forefinger.
Sight line, white lines,
riding the hiss-hot rails to a place of Federal care.

Antelope headgear of a mimic
spear-carrier.
A verbal trail discarded by
military intelligence is
interference pattern:
leopard's spots against
tree foliage
blinking with sun.
Antique stalker skills bagging
a far political organisation.

One hand on the bottle and one . . .
Andy sitting out at night with a Midwest blonde.
Andy's square dancing drill squad pissing testosterone
Slapping heel and toe with the Hessian.
Steadily losing arguments with the Devil.
Rolling in *the Surrey with the fringe on top*
Andy knocking in stakes and lines in Strassmeir County,

Buying federally restricted rounds by fedEx.
Andy kickin' back. Andy digging Western Swing.
Andy fading up the patches of blur.
A lurk in the lurch. Damned straight, in the straddle.

The Ghost of Fusion

bambalam, Shambhala
bonanza in Utah

The dirty liquid of language
pinched by zero flow
isotropically radiant
without decrease of noise.
A peer network
not capillary
in a glittering spray
of vapourised palladium

It doesn't work!
and the Japanese already have it!!
Congress doesn't dicker
with five big ones

From fusion to leak
via writs, patents, and flashes
to start with vindict and finish with verdict
a room with no people
is an illusionless room

Helium-3 boils up from
rock flaws
in the mountains
above Bengal; problems of diffusion
from a thermal vent on the seabed
or a chink of improbity
The catalyst outperforms the analyst;
international mirror setups show
that wicking in solids is a site for
interpolation. We see only heat
in the new Short-Lived Products Wing
dedicated to
observer-funder

interactions.
A pond where the curious
dunk the canard
about tritium being cheaper than canards
in the forward tariffs

The starvation of the wishes
by a scaled background
a concept mapped more exactly
onto itself by radial
flow, or, zero wriggle.

foofaraw, jamboree
gas cheap as water
power for free

The Shield of Perseus

The colour of silence
neurological shimmer, the density of the air
fine silver needles about to shake.
A kind of drink called the *fins écarts*, or
sequence rules for reading a room—
A forestallers' viewing of
                mondain intelligentsia,
                        skincare of the selfware,
The popular front of lurking
                aesthophanous autonomarchs
                    and gainsaying exquisites,
Writing to the script which writes
                an invisible public score, or,
tautologous honorifics
                from spoils to favours—
plucking tender leaves
            of competitive morality.
Me too
      spinning steadily
           to impress one's rivals
I'm one of these happy few.
The phantom of beautiful language
is tempted by the space they stress
and lock as offsets are defined as peaks.

On the shield I watch my actions
at 0.5 second's delay, stiff and shiny,
a screen of warrantable optic quality,
holding five minutes of extent, a graphic
alloy scanning grain edges & wave apices.
My facial planes heaving in
vagueness over a
rigid gaze of horror brightened by
swells of rage where a
mime of benevolence
is momentary and sinister.

As with languid scruples the buffet of assets
is seized and flaunted
by solicitors of the self and power grocers
he rehearses and rejects an utterance
before a panel probing for flaws of drafting.
Wearing the teeth of deceased professors,
reciting paradoxes in blocks of 7 and 13 syllables,
they set him out and cut him down.

Visible tremor of limbs
where discordant states flow over a shared surface
between a fit and a trance
he sets out his stall once more.

The discretion of women, like an aromatic. This pointless task
of being unhappy proves
the staging of a conversation
with plebeian effort
          to such attractive victims
                 of low-altitude
                 blurts
"I've got it now, a thousand
acts of petty vindictiveness become
a millimetrical
scale of nuances,
the ego enriched by fine scars
into a frill?" At this point
no-one wants to be standing near him.
Social life
now starts some years of obligate recesses.

Starved by the feast at
seeing two other people in love
She experienced the moment of aura and admired herself experiencing it
where the desire to imitate them
makes all the litigation files start reciting at once
a tragedy no larger than a bath.

Martyrdom and Triumph of Sergei Korolev

The year is 1938,
The slave states glut on their gold and steel,
The entities of rage eat the living faces.
If the few forgot,
In the projects of lies and homicide, if they lost,
Faint, vengeful and overcome,
Part of the sparse lines of civility, stripped and chilled,
Stricken from the senses,
Who could bring it back?

Where the Kolymà River flows towards the Northern Ocean;
In the Zone of crime and atonement
Korolev dreamed of the paths to a new world.
In the astronomical belt of scarcity,
The staging zone towards metabolic
Death, spectres dig for gold in frozen soil. Where
The planet ceases, the cosmos
Trails its meshes of death and variation.
A nacelle streaks across Arctic skies.

Where minds must go first, K.
Dreams the divisions of fineness.
The stardown is wrapped and protected by their
Weightless reckoning, sensory planes peeled away,
Sheared, pegged, attenuated
For the serials of a new mechanics.
Body images
Falling through the reds and yellows of dawn;
A forest grows metal hulls,
Birch shafts shot through the track of the upper air.
He launches his fleets and watches their chances
Wiped in thousands, the error trailed and netted in the other
  sky.
His upshot makes a gravity wall loose as sand.
The nozzle is a muzzle of waste heat;
In a vacuum, it adjusts the course.

Like spires, minarets, columns, AA shells. A
Principle of ascent smooths and tapers the dream object.
Like earths, charcoal ovens, blast furnaces, breeches, bombs:
Chambers into which substances flow, and where they change.
The planet of sound, the Mach-1 surface, the tune of discharge
Resonance, singing the craft out of the air. The muffles
Which rifle an explosion
From a sphere
Into a linear discharge
On course for the boundless slightness.

He dreams of the ghost of intelligent behaviour, a shell which
Alters shape to keep its course. Three gyros on three axes
Describe the orientation of their platform: x, y, z. Cased off
From local influences, at the moment of exit they're looking for
Gravity which isn't there. He knows the place: a desert close to
The Equator. The time—close to dawn, the trackers can see the
Round in high contrast, as if slowed, out from co-axial

Streaks
        of fuel and
                friction sparks.

Diffuse
        clarity
                wiped over

A featureless,
        equable,
                range.

The fluid substance of dawn draws its curve.
The human star races meteorites over the sand of Tyuratam.
A treader on emptiness, drinker of fire,
Whose eyes follow the sun and the moon.
Lightness razed a fletched titanium shell,
A tensed mouth caught the phonology of an explosion.
Rear the arch with no ground, scan the metre with no fall.

Where all the numbers of fire are bent from their vagrance
The slender spire ascends on heroic furies.
The lattice of snow and sunshine is thrown wide, the shatterer
Of forts unmasks his ordnance:
In the latitude whose sky flashes out of the arrow
The polisher of meteorites gazes through etched glass at cerebral
    fire.

The year is 1956. Korolev unlatches the sky.

In the nine lands of the Kolymà
An engineer is thrown down a mine shaft, the frozen ground
Refusing State corpses. Laid-by by the stere.
Was it all bluster? impossibles
Left in from mere self-love, lyric nights
Scribbling wide figures? some provincial genius
Laying out a new social system? The docket
Was never filed. The dying
Recite the names of the dead. Snowflakes
Fall to pick up a wink of heat
And draft up, vanishing in plain sight.

8 ROY FISHER

from The Cut Pages

~

To origin, which is another patch of sun. We are shown another patch. Not the one. Was the one we tried to look for not the one, whereas this is? Perpetually displaced. Or is this what can be seen, the surrogate, while the true one cannot be perceived?

Skirting it. We must have crossed it many times. Hard to say. There is nothing that has to be done with regard to it

Monstrous love

Shaggy fragments sailing out of the background

Into the drop-sheet, or past it. There's a sheet hangs to catch things, but maybe it doesn't. Nothing sticks

Ferreting, by the handfuls, in among what was left. Not one scrap demands to be kept more than the other

The opening is much deeper, but it doesn't matter

Everything is changed. Without warning. Everything *was* a warning

The slipping foot. The cry. The gap trapped in the opening

Sedbergh. With all the escape roads removed, obliterated

Altered. Men alter. Are altered

Everything in the street runs to the end, to the open space where there's always movement

A type of sky at the street's end where there seemed to be shapes of giant arches, as if from that particular place on the world changed into one where there were such arches

Some war long before. Not one of the wars of time. In the dream-time. Some war learned of before time was learned The operators of the war were of their own world, not an earlier generation of this

Rose-stuff, the variations: whisked, turning

Back, fanning up the line, past the starting place, back on another track, with mud motion, slow progress. To be seen, at all costs

Not located in ice, or mud, or flat plane. In air or glass. Counter-system that won't engage in a dialectic

Far. It is far from us. No. We are far

With that, everything has come to us in a cluster. Turn it inside out, and step out of it. Call for another

Separations, a rhythm of trenching the moving mass, that reforms round the suggestions. The rhythm separates. The spaces are alive

Always falling to be away, never on the rise

Away, travelling: to come upon whatever rises, distends, is bland and broad in the ruck

Voyage is through partial things, mixtures, edges where tangled
solidities give on to broken-up vacancies

Stump. Ampetus stump

The ceilings ran on, through arch after arch. The floors had been
furnished anyhow, with islands and dams of clutter

Have you seen anybody?

They're everywhere—of a kind

The text of fury, with oncoming plumes, the orb of darkness, the
fire-feathers

Yes. Those are the steps. Down around the outside of the curved
wall. No, it's not in nature; you're right

Friends surround me

Lower than the treetops all about, there is the ground, the false
floor. Always to be going down, arrested and spread, only to run
wide, looking for an edge to what's down

Red blush, swelling at the middle and mottling across

Perpetual Check depends on the alternation of moves between the
players. The opponent has no way of selling you an extra move,
whatever price you offer. But there's some aspect of the game
that's in a position to make the offer, and there's a price it will
accept

Price!

Interviews, breaking away into riots round the house. Stripped up
the wallpaper, all the old intentions

The mill. Opens everything out above, white frames, the bright things open. It's all right. The good will die, they will come to us. Spread of the sails, the angles where they meet at the boss, the places where they straddle to the full, the places from which they could be broken inwards towards each other

Elm. The mouth

Separated, it still had life, the break looking like nothing and all that was alive in it sticking out brightly. The wilting bitter and sharp, curses with no possibility of contradiction

What a wish is. Like a broad nipple. Like a place in the trees, distant, boxed-off, dull. I want that because it's mine

Nowhere to head for. Nothing to be done. This discontinuity is my discontinuity

One patch of town has noticably more wires about than any of the others. Only coincidences

The head of it: up into the height. A hardening of style, but nothing more

When I am going I shall wish—what a wish is. The elm

The wrong side of a door, the ladder standing away from the wall at the top

Turning the place again, it finds trees and a pond. A dead crow like a fish burnt in the pan lodged in a bush by the water

The blind is lowering all the time and the world dives with it, answering with brilliance bursting from the glass

Red hook, red smoke powder. The comedian with dusty stockings and flat belly drum

Soft white pointed peppers

Wire print arrangements rushing through, fence disputes on order

The holes are made, reamed about till the core's exposed. The answers will drop in

Laws for the empty. Patterns for the free

A leaf shape hangs like a wheel against the light, with rings of holes cut in it. Stemmed and attached to others, and springing from a dark main stalk. Many such heads hanging about the stalk

Past a simple shed

On to blue bricks, flat

Against blue bricks, standing

A flight of domes below

There is addition, there is flight. There is the simple state that is always tilting, easily but always. If you go with it you can hold, if you neglect to you're thrown

Clothing rich but fusty, beaded with hard things. Kept in the bottom of a room, dusty velvet, dusty sun

To rely on the spongy disc in the floor, with its concentric ridges. The floor holds if the disc gives. It gives and presses back

It will be barbaric, the middle channel between the squares

Cannot be said

Cannot be caught

Gone into a detail. A forked detail. A cluster. A generality

Sold out; and the price thrown after it

Cold canvas; naked in the cold canvas, vulnerable to thought but protected in every possible way by everybody

By certain people. Certain knees, feet, hands, necks, ears. Faces, never. Voices in discussion. The word was corrupt. The word corroded

The plant seemed more permanent than the man

The sun is written on from the other side

Miraculous urine, streaming among the ice. The boot, the snaky hulls against the murk. Deep tanned brown of the swept pavement between the snowfields. Earth solid with black fire, sky with grey fire

Soon

The streams ran through the garden round the house and in under the balconies. In some of the rooms there were channels of running water bridged by plank walks from which the plants trailed

Serpentine roads in such bare scrub they weren't hidden one from another. More roads than there were reasons for

Holding the hair over the distance

Silence. Silent water. Feed the sounds into the silence. Sun. Grey sun. Track sun

The painted wheels hum in the early morning. Grey pigeons are lit from beneath

The rim. To a great distance. Eaten back to the least nothing but
the bare curve. Utterly without excrescence

Subject. Measure a subject. See which way it sticks out. How it's
fixed, and to what

9 LIONEL G. FOGARTY

By Accident, Blinked

We sharing children, visit near mocking
led fresh country town.
Sentencing narcotic evil spit.
Wristed excellence, disbelief clouded quickly in mud
Sandflies bleed, corroborees unknowing bluegum
even sunrise cries.
Digging naked skulls sneaked along, so no greedy victories
Blackboy sided of a hill
women bad placed, cause him say bones wrong
Bitumen cursed, dated gloom, supremed over a dream.

The swan moans and crash glasses, spinning wheels
an accident polished neat
fails giving, 'help we, help me'.
Worry shot congeals pretty screams
in throat, a note. Curve skeleton coated a modern blink of life
Lost stemming flattened hearts
conventioned abandoned, sounding
rinsed craze giggled smiles
leaves worms sides unstrived
Pity rockets burst combined
yearn behind everyones locked intergrating.
My stand platitudes a smell
clinged kind and signed
so don't fade a halt glassless stare at recompense
we windmills it.

Memory foolish fantasy
flecks heartache cheating
our hatch mortality, freedoms in uplift
and indigenous.

Am I

Am we lonely these days
Am I grief in the wind
Am us friend to nature
well hooked me up and
we'll fish
The dreamed dreams are
opened for wishes to come to life
Am you hurt
Am you to see me
We am and dem gonna
sleep and dreams of my people
There all alone in the mind
Murri stranger came to me
and said, Am I the one outside
you all getting spiritfully
When sun shines in the rains
we find summer here sooner
Treat my mother with a career
Treat conscience with rotten
education
Women are allowing bodies to
be taken
At last moment of life
Love even nobly came
against my skin
I heard a roo cry
Am I hearing attendants
to my hearts
Am we lovin' in these days
Am I sadden these nights
Forever it possess you man
something must tell
Am I me or you am us.

Memo to Us (story)

Fortunately Australia has been given back to Aboriginals now.

I'm sorry to tell you your passport is out of date, you must all leave this place. QLD is no more yours, white queen of England, it's been given to the natives. NSW has been deserted by the whites for some time now, the blacks have taken over. Tasmania is run by blacks who ran the devils out, and VIC is total abo control, so gubba have not got even a batman chance. SA is taken by forceful music singer blacks, and the whites are gone. They just didn't want a tribal law. WA blacks destroyed all modernised houses and put the poor together with the rich, over there no white power runs. The NT, has changed all faces, tongues to blackfella.

Now here in Australia no white race lives, they are lost at sea and sent to spaces. So it took not long to restore all the natural things back to life. So it began to flower with new love, dreaming and sharing and care. The lands turn to paradise, beautiful rivers, hills, soil rose to greet the aboriginal race. Happy the days they hunted for food, greatly aboriginals respected each tribes. On forever, the land was filled and re-filled with behaviour of loving their own.

Yes, this time the migglou made a mistake by giving us the land back. Then us, we aboriginals all garden for a ceremony.

One tribe stood up proud and said, 'we are land, we have re-lived and we have beaten, killed the whites, but are we humans? We got to let them back to live.' Then out came a painted white man dancing a dance they did at pubs.

Of course all the blackfellas clapped, saying and danced, 'til the dawn awoke with the sun showing the colouring of many a day so wonderful. The time came at the fire to eat the goanna, roos, fruitnuts and other things. Everyone was so full, they laid under the biggest tree for a rest before going home. At noon the aboriginals all thanked each other, then off they went in their peaceful surroundings. From the sea up above came a poor ghostly sound saying, 'I mean my race to do you abos no desecration, we are the white ones whose city roaring homes

are gone, but will you please, oh aborigines, let us back to live in harmony with youse.' All the abos said: 'look white race if, and dats a big IF, we let you back you must obey one rule, never be greedy. And anyhow, our new world is without the things you need, like wars. Oh migglous, go on, find your souls, that's what you gotta do.'

At this time the poor old migglou ghostly sound faded into infinity. By now all Aboriginals were cooeeing cooee voices up and up so their spirits won't tire again. Now Australia is living in a heavenly camping home for all aboriginals. Of course, you whites out there are spaced pigs out into a time unknown. But us Aboriginals have the new stone age and science knowledge to bring you back to earth. Oh well, this part of land anyway. Immense and credible to your mind. But this one thing all abos think.

Kath Walker

We are coming, even going
I was born in 1957
the year after I became a realist
I am a full blooded black Aussie
we want racialism
you got ostracism
black ascendance
Charter of Rights, she said
Hey, now they got dependents
exploitation is being done here
Self-reliance, not compliance
most will say, resign
circumscribe the enemy, not befriend
they will give oversight and
human segregationary rights.
No choice. No colour conscious.
Give us bigots who are not biased
Give us prevention, not ambition
Status, not condescension.
Give us Lord Christ and confidence
all we do is fellowship bureaucratic protection.
Give me settlements, camped in missions
Prohibition
from old, young time.
Thank you. Education makes us equals
Opportunities are disheartening
we defend white over-lordship
rebuff the independence
my laws ain't no cold choice.
Native, old salvation seller
we are the conquerors to take over
not Christ
So our land in law

must rank out aliens
in our banished race
though you baptised by
Just black . . .

Fuck All Departments

I takin' our comparative mis-saying
Down south of the law blacks roam
The dialect is harder to vocab
if you don't know.
Up south laws and the Dep. Abo Affairs
were like here.
Pick stealing our Koori Murri brains
where you sit, fire warmth
are you to set fire to buildings
so white, so right.
The Housing Co-op worker was fielding
in areas of gubba mentality
by making us pay rent on black own land
they say our Ha. Ha.
The bastards just like gubba
You can't give blackfella house
when him break, smash windows
walls, rip floors. Knock fences
down for wood.
For fire is our saving
electric bills . . . ha. ha. you black
Thinkin' migglou
Community controls means you don't
go National meeting swearing
declare war on governments
just your ways.
Everybody differ level
understanding family wantin' own
Ship was and is here now, this year
The money have to be spent by
the already set-up community operating
I'm staying in Department for a while
Well go fucken live in Canberra
Big money . . . junga you after hey?
Binna hearing conditions drawn by the gubba
pass down to you clowns

But been going around
This Jacky Jacky surrounded
Poor poor Koori
who getta caught
You come.
I yell hate, if let this community
go out of balance.
Get out of this gubba affairs
Ours await no more
We must fight you cunts too . . .
Truly open the public eye
open the party public servants
to black intervention
so we can clear you all out.
Again forces voiced by young people
must come out of age fully
Just better watch Koori persons
You smoking drinking don't speak
I'm into my community units
Us gotta concept of man
organised ability
Aboriginality is a very powerful
knowledge
of us . . . Ha . . . Ha . . .
All the best for Koori family
single you must feel
Department blacks you word-play
too much
a Koori term you selling south
Abuse us even when you office desk
push pens to get rid of us.
Justice shines with we people
Cos fightin' to fuck up
Dep. Abo airing saying
'I'm doing my best for my people'
jumper outer place when we pinpoint you
Telling truth. Them shit themself
Maybe we intimate your meeting

for our sake.
Light the burri.
Hear our Koori law.
Departments we destroy.

Biral Biral

Biral came down one day
crystal stones went where none would dare.
Just a little boy, known by everyone
send a flower picked for this one, time expressed
Reply had to be made, springs invoked
'Who is Biral?'
Walking alone sharp rocks cut my feet
leaf push upon my skin.
Bad tribes were known to never return
greatest healthful huge size spirit
enters manhood
taking violence away
fading in a day.
Morally, I'm not better off.

Ngunda supreme. Live spirally in my being.
Death inflicts existence
too real for this world.
Supernatural customs differ to human
now tribes who have lives on
fellow of the nameless kind.
Journeys, new born, mixture powder
a virility more wonderful than risks.
Magic escape compassion, no good to say.
Space veined howls around knowledge, bitter gift
the sucking bloodless fed strong men
feared in homeless whirl, by passwords.
Ambush admitted the tunnel of music
entered the little boy now known by everyone
Trumpeted the didgeridoos
operaed a stranger calls.
Speaking souls, race blows weird things onto faces
made u'fella look like creatures of another era.
Sweet simple bodies, paths shadows
dazzled masked ritual and religion.

She turned, asking her people
I've never seen Ngunda
So why show a boy meaning nothing
a little boy, smaller than an ant
looking for a fight with porky pines.
My answer shattered in storms.
and disposed in scrubs where none haunts
and where river parts inside my guts
for I am 'belief'.

Beauty, parents may protect helpless creeping country babies
but will they point the way to waterhole.
Mountains lazy survived future dispensed
cause land felt slaughter to any who lifeless the hills
Fish and snake rest, while people eat rope
they hung themselves.
Wicked terrific scenes came
diversity sensational, all down the tracks at night.
This relationship I previously had, shorter
now it longer
so however highest degree or what the spirit dwells
deep and contemporary in us
it is within
Watching morning asleep
but gunya, sparkling stars windowed at darkness
a giggle swept tears
winning a day and night
no a stomach tight and empty, crawling
search a prey over near grasses
shapes stretched to marvel
then dreaming forced Mum, Nanna and lotta people
shouting, me to sing out
Weakness no more
Ngunda
Biral
Many influences, many spirits

Nguthuru too.
These words, not vocation
Born, inbred by Aboriginal people
I'm blood. Sheer and delightful.

17/11/82

~~fragmento~~

angle anatomy
anywhere
jade jawed
within an abundantly green interior
quick drying
plants glisten fresh dust
lines and veins smudged into binding
bank the flora bargain
held up
lapwing from traffic
stanza flutter
air conditioned climes provide
a pacing cooler
a barrenness
until driven through
burning visa
risk a whisper
lisp deterrer fracture radio
tannoy

a curt snarl
dusts corrupted
towed tweeds
how the policy rusted
clasps closed spine

held a caller
peak pack

                                                            ante
                                        purse sharing stake brilliant
                        diapered to form

        to disappear
to take underground
    border spared

                    compacts finals

                                        decadence debt synchronise
                        swank with sunk

                                dwelled dilettante dimension passion
                    graft on lying in close association
                                        on the face of it survive ledge
                            flexed at elbow
                            fine sandy old trackway
found writing at speed
    in

    a
                            state
                        of dental eruption corporates
                            with no hairstyle
                            snapped lifestyle
uniformity sun-up
    superficially sloping down
spirals close twist
    worsted garment weave
    sleep rivets
        these socket accounts
    scribe any attachment missing cut away
    roar becomes a snore
                        in the dream
                        roaming rim of river

                                light-headed linger lost grip and collapse
                                amethyst lifeless ornament via pager
                                        out of business

                                                    [83]

                                              closed sign on fist

                    mud may buy lining of a luminous wall
                          and mouth movie much
                          backward animations
            whilst nervy neighbours crack the clay settled upon
                        hang from flower box plateau
                an everyman chateau as rules of engagement
        marketing marriage
    darkening passage

                                              no further ornamentation
                                                           to the verge
                                                            overhanging
                                                                longing

    altitude an ambiguous impression
                          bookie bake palpations
                              marks in money
                             funny it pierced
                                  bodies

                                    terminal rendezvous manoeuvres
                                           a controversial stare
                                                      forgiven
                                   a panic struck lover's fingerprint
                                           estimated ghost spinning
                                               meaning once gave
                                           another colour to hands
                                               clouds to weep to

    prints a goodbye replica repack
                covered with an inky membrane
                          night at the pit apertures
                          prepared from surface
                                              while from within
                        sigh & heave anchor
                             as a mariner dangled rope
                          breathe a cap size

& come spring may i counting
knot response look in each wave
lends a splintered solar system
shards of light cut to darkness lost ash
whilst paper crumbles before eyes
with whom according
law of attraction
a two body prescribed
one weightless
as though need
scrolled upon faceplate
fissures
between visor views
relay relationship dependence
an invention intention
a map of conserve you
eludes folding
and shreds an air of blown
speed well fingered
outlying

rows of spruce yellow dry
that rattle branches
to greater skylark scatters
mirage of urban conifers
cones & dishes

cypresses for cynics
transport decay exposing obsolescence
got the dress sense
inversion triads moving in parallels
thickening a melodic line
attachment plates damage
depression on broad facade
and skin also present
narrow voice reception
touching slowed with aversion
display validity blocks parity checking
a babble band response

over talk bandage
remote iron central
semi-detached behind hard wire
get micro scratched from filings
feel the force textured intervals doubling
clear period tongue contacting
in an originator non-chord tone
conceivable paid reason
lips magnetic

density impulse specific
skin presented said

night scented
blue lobelia
crystal palace
fountain mix trailing

dug in
upright
disturbance roots
reorienting
spacing option collapse
where any interfacing fixed
answer back message fades
to doors disintegrating
a mode code excluded
free from deduction
its plain opening
in a layered white
flakes
a padded appearance
curves backing cotton
seeking indigo blurs
blue abundance
blink of an eye blisters certayne drawings
a wizen circumference networks
experience to hold down emotion
stagnation drops the skin stone undertow

a paranoid status penetrating trust latitudes
pulse vehement in pieces bolt enclaves
a gentrified fallout limehouse rail links
cough a nonchalant air a choke grief partying
understatement dipped in polyurethane foam
of
bracing
akin
thrust
regulated in a made up base
in an armchair suspended
above sighting well flecked
meet pitted
all verticals embellishment for household
highly yarn
enclose a centre block
articulates rosettes
dyed deep recurring

yet makes a screen acceptable veneer
burnt oak polish bitter wormwood
beats old in hot constitutions
comes portable double spy bear purging well
contaminates itch frontiers steel elements
headrest various positions
appropriate table lamp directed shade trade eyes

compartmentalised sound wave wraps
robotic large screw sturdy
tripod traditional respectability violence
elasticity
a scream
to mute

wiped smoking glass facilitates
lens prison out paced
in hoodwink fancy
a derivative notion

[87]

where heart hooked horizontal
yet visualise vivacious
with anonymous grasping
waive or entwine
from tempo heard impulsive
puffs a fluffed fibre glass insulation insecurity

illusion windows

to a set light consumption

from floor to ceiling assumes

views

floated deviation bathes

a pre-set neck zipper an endurance plus

glided with rust in a foil speedway suit

beside the titles squeezed between shelving

partial expenditure written across

bar code

a unit of closeness

that merely scans yearns

locking acquisition in

a step shut-down

screening out breathing in
lock into green eyes
salt up these words

in the nasa space dictionary

read on swallowed tablets

lived by
divert your variety
red lead mixed
most potent line
swan expressing

books
to

                                                    bonfire
                                                    before
                                                    my eyes
                                                    from beetles
                                                    to farmyard
                                                    machines
                                        heighten your stalks to talks
                                                give a slight wash
                                                    of carmine
                                        have cybernetic quivers

& comments upon
  shewn the nature
      catalogue smells
      geranium manner
    of delicacy
    & extremely
proceed to another
  twilight zero

                            medium modem
                            sugar coat enrich

      told which must be done gallstone
          overcooked lettuce to wipe nerve ends

                            liquid purple agreeably deep stipple
                                                    upon them
                                                    friday
                                    stranded some concrete beech
                                                    & tarmac
                                                    reaching

                            described background by chewing out
                                                a stare mortars
                                                    pointedly
                                        crouched in doorway
                                                expanding chest
                                                hyperventilated

between knot of an unopened parachute
tangles a heart jump
small island
having a square
to wander

many lines crossing vital
a medium sized hand

barely held feather
lets go touch
moulted scribble
repel meaning pressed
never occurred petal
from the leg
of table
this margin requires capital
starkly additives trading
storm residue
shoe prints in an oral bite mark
in a few good steps noted
explicit motion
germ buckle total
diagram moon with function glove
clutch a wall nozzle
load down references
crude potassium
a fine grained deflection
extinguish
a reverse depiction
in
sampler patched triangulations
lacquer
illuminates
drawers
pulled right
muscles on stone less cherry
empty stage eyes and body floats around upside-down world

limbs stretched

splits across hemispheres

edge opposite

gums

next lime

crystal solid engagements

drop frog making connections

bids and blossom heads pine

brushed sign

maze like spots

wax flows from document

a convenient passage of oak carving

wrecks brackets where light flows in

pencil to lips sap green

flatlands application of telepresence

cut off by dense growth pressure

changing at bottom of the ocean ordnance chance

or cameras or whatever

headphones be a welding torch

change in ray brightness dance

look at building

to see a red horse

11 PETER GIZZI

Lonely Tylenol

There I could never be a boy
FRANK O'HARA

You have to begin somewhere.
The devil of your empty pocket moves as escargot
up the artery of a hollow arm,
ending on the lip of your dismay—it shows—
in the Brillo morning of a shaving mirror.
It is that morning always, and it is that morning
now, and now you must fight, not with fists
but with an eraser. The duelist awaits a ham sandwich
on the dock where your ship comes in.
Be warned and without ceremony take your place
as you have before. Only look once
at the idiot chagrin and smile as you ready your slingshot.
You are not alone in your palindrome.
Why is it so hard to know everything it said
when the mirror spoke. The book is darker
than night. Do you read me?
This is written somewhere and no one can
read it. It is not for them but to you
it is a reproof from years of neglect.
There there. No place like home.

Another Day on the Pilgrimage

There is an I in space, I am, space
where a sparrow falls. Who can tell it?
When goodbye is the operative word
forgiveness is either easy or impossible.
Looking into your eyes I see more
than I came to address. The morning
the car lit out. That first memory
each time I die. Then is the world shut down
for a while. Hoping to meet again
some other day, hoping for the refrain
to conduct us all into a neighborhood
not furtive, but rich with color
and the telling of lost cities they leave never.
Place, this generating question
only answered when the orange drops,
that is twilight, becomes a kiss.

What are those sounds in the dark?
Can they tell of our lives, can they
begin to unfold the pain in the eye,
the slow girth of the long night.
There are crowds gathered with faces
pressed up against the sill, so many
faces at the sill. I wish I could tell them
what we are and where we are going.
Instead the blue interval and the open plain,
this green wedge and the brown hill.
Tell me, can I say *who* or can I
say *now*? And will words awaken
the desire to know, to push open the nerve.

The green book on the blue bed has answers.
It tells of our need for description, the apex
where nerve net and hair stem meet
and expose wind or express time between

the sheets. I have a paper cut on my finger
it smarts when I push off to feed. Turn
the page to diagram 4, a box and an outline
of a cape, together they articulate—grain,
thorn and shoes—they equal a figure.
Tiresias on an open road reading signs.
The dead are useful he said
to tell us where we are. This is a hard hat area.
The image of the spectator trapped
in a mirror, the relationship of spectator, object
and the space within love's bent axis.

Will you quit that banging?
Like a sullen barber the blade of the season
mows down the last buds and you find yourself
without pajamas. The balloon ascends
throughout the years and the view
only gets less colorful and distant. O where
are my tin toys and first books and the sun
is no longer new? The pages of the book are smooth
and yet you can climb the face of narrative
carefully and with great ardor. The one flower
on the cliff face will be yours if you persist.
The wind continues to interpret the story
as the old latch is gone from the back door—
whoosh and bang all evening
makes one's nerves sharpen to the point
of a syringe. I like how autography is geologic
or geographical. All my people have larger bodies.
Will you compare me to a pyramid or a clover
in the trash? When I am inscribed to tell
of the beauty of innuendo
I am like unto a feather—quick.

When the skiff returns from its solo
each night the organism is renewed.
Nameless moments our destiny.

So many leaves to unfurl. Later to be
reinscribed in a second tongue
we call grammar, we call and call forever
to the next page. The speech in boxes.
Little caskets of ventriloquism tell
our plight, explain our confusion
and generally identify our loneliness here
on the surface. What it was would be
like this. How small and how nothing.
Cathedral light only in memory.
Immemorial space smiles, blurs
the template before the impression
is made. The artifact in time fades
and we are left with a blank slate.
We are left, it is that simple.

The robes lie in a rebus on the shore
where the beloved sang,
thwarted into nothing. Thwarted.
No embellishment please, the day
is sufficient. Who could tell, as all
the listeners' ears are stoppered with their
own invention. A carbuncle ascends
like a gray morning is a body?
The opium eaters have erased their eyelids.
An absorbed earth is altered, fallow
and gusts of stinging filth pierce us
as we move from moment to task.

Later the voice stripped laughter's heft
and became a mottled chronology.
You haven't moved an inch. *Know it.*
Twirl. Until drawing all rumor
into your coterie you exhaust the actual
breeze which is our inheritance, not
the small fires you, squatting, tend.
Right activity is the only promise

twinned with the natural processes of earth.
That's where you can find me,
carrying my bundle for the pyre?

Road, sing the changes your geometry gives.
Recondite lines projecting
into revisionist fields at dawn.
A wobbling moon imitates a mouth
in mourning. These gestures caught in blue light
become a context become carved upon
all features enacted in sleep.
A tiny voice has begun to sing the background
of everything the foreground blurs.
Ecstatic in its trill and because we seek
less and settle for more its swell
will burst us in our distracted way,
our mortgaged fear, adumbrated in kind.

Fables of Critique

You are not outside this film (or movie)

Without a subject a page signals to no one

You are not outside a field (or yard)

Unable to wake free from the tall grasses

Several grasses yield a specific poison

These leaves are not pretty, they are camouflage

You are outside now and they were the enemy

Those brambles and thickets are not shallow

Refusing to enclose the area, they cannot be buried

You are pleased you are no longer a child

And standing by a building (decomposing)

Several films descend from the sky

Here was (were) the grass (grasses)

Ignoring you they bother no one

You are no longer a man standing by a building

Where no one came you are not waiting

No one came, no one wasn't there

They are no longer a child, no longer a subject

Nothing is a film (movie)

Which is becoming your eyes

You are (were) unable to speak

And now you were before them

They become impatient (becoming impatient)

And this is (was) your future

Last Cigar

A ball drops from a high place, its orbit spent.
If it were that simple they'd've already called
the dogies home for supper. End of story.
Instead the workers are scattered wide
upon the plain, stuck in their own voice-over.
Listen. One is carried upstream,
another further off into distant steam,
some remain in one place while others
hurtle equally through space. Buckshot
across a field. A sharp cackle spoils the breeze.
They sure were busy out there
ignoring the triangle's gay tinkle.
It's like this every night, the reporter
casually smiled. What could they be doing
forever? The boss came round from time to time
to make sure no one of them actually came
to anything, anything close to anything,
that is, and the ambiguity between somewhere
and nothing, something and nowhere
was maintained. It's a beautiful thing
the song sang, "smoke in your eyes," right?

Tous les Matins du Monde

Goodness is hard on the body,
a distracted mind unable to doze in fitful sleep.
The dove rattles the mind into thinking
it has a body of thought—complete
& symbolic—the gray feathers perched
outside the pale cut square of silver.
Say then, we belong to that window,
that warble, and suddenly we belong too,
the silver car in the yard, even a tiny silver hammer.
All vehicles of travel
disclose the mind's need to wonder in perfect forms.
Even if the skiffsman don't come to this bed
to rock me to sleep—to wander the tired stones again
and worn teeth we remember to hold onto a world
for this life might not take us the whole way.
That shape of an idea, the concept, or *donnée*
travels farther than the instrument can register.
The spindle whirs beyond its order.
Something must be moving at incredible speed.
With pure speed I address you, reality.

Ding Repair

There are too many skateboards here, too many
waves to negotiate, the graded hills fall
too suddenly into the sea; from here
that bank of fog turns into a blanket of gauze,
never forgetting anxiety—institutions
are a part of nature though needs
are seldom met in a sunny bureaucracy,
shiny country, for the moment sun-bleached.

Imagining another home far from here
not from where we have come but where we imagine,
where vulnerability won't reproduce cruelty.
A home in the act of finding a home in the act of
what will suffice? No place was set
at the table but you are invented to listen
even if silence is a condition of mind
you will never be forgotten here, where to learn
the speech of the place is to earn to speak in this place.

Said: "I could love you if you left me?"
"No! I will love you if you let me."
Things come to them, a tuning fork
pulling focus, facing each other at breakfast.
Outside sea and sky enlarge the chamber piece,
little flowers dot the hills, for they too
are a part of themselves, parts of themselves
scattered—stuck to cars and windshields.

A hummingbird at the scarlet bell works the vine.
Even as adults we hope to witness ordinary spectacle
evolve into meaning, ordinary and rare each time
the ribbon, the wave—all bent.
For if those memos, phone calls, holidays
were to accrue then where would we be?

If a letter were drafted it would read
the people are cheerful, overworked and kind.
Say there is plenty ocean, plenty sun.
Say we are standing on a new shore
that goes to—if not new—different destinations.
Say these destinations trouble us at night.
There's work to do, faces to study.

Some of the news contains lack—
say the small charge from a battery—
in this way a current flows, querulous
even, a lighthouse has its seasons too.
The metaphor is striking
however like a match making the dark
darker, the night larger
the empty into which we move real.

And holding your hands over your head
reflecting a degraded self-portrait
feel the cord of space pass through your palms
the slow progression of years, endless knots and bits
of talk, lumps of sorrow, nettling of tears.
Close your eyes and find the present flattened.

To speak about distance, memory
a voice stumbles, a flame in wind
when dignity is no longer an option
and rain does not confuse
—folding themselves against the night
into night, or just wearing out the day.

Let the record play, let the notes begin
to make a landscape where we meet beneath
the intermittent sky, let the body evolve whole
rising out of the throat and out of the mouth into night.
Pick up an instrument, play, as though a work of art
were a form, C 38, here fill this out, as though we must behave
as we explain the mess we've made, one note

for citizen, soldier, object, history, but there is no other
door to enter and if there were where would you go
after the masterpiece is finished?

Or a man who can't distinguish the sorrow of the violin
from rust of the old country.
The day sallow and dry leans to the left
the trill accentuates the bulbous tops of trees
out over the terrace, everything in its nest
each unlike each along the jagged edge of horizon
the strings of the instrument articulate each spear
of big ferns across the parking lot.

It is a song that carries this day
yields to the shy, lays its bluster down
tucks in the storms, a new tune atonal for the moment
until the small have grown to embody it.
As though the entire armature
were labeled "heavens" reproduced
inside the home we call our heads
—a ship in a bottle.
Hole inside in the shape of a bottle.

Now when you go to your job, your table or your bed
can you remember this place, a piece
of space left behind, it's not hard to imagine.
Think of an empty closet, some childhood there
an odor of cedar, order of secrets repeat
their sequence and the useless treasure of an ending.

12 LYN HEJINIAN

The Beginner

This is a good place to begin.

From something.

Something beginning in an event that beginning overrides.

Doubt instruction light safety fathom blind.

In the doorway is the beginning thus and thus no denial.

A little beat of time, a little happiness quite distinct from misery as yet.

The sun shines.

The sun is perceived as a bear, then a boat, then an instruction: see.

The sun is a lily, then a whirlpool turning a crowd.

The shadows lengthen, the sun-drenched line of arriving strangers are all admitted, seen in the day and not the same at night, host and guest alike.

Two things then, both occurring as the beginner arrives: acceptance and the reconstruction of the world which that acceptance implies.

In the first twenty-four hours nearly blind and with hands swelling, the gaze fierce, face scowling, the beginner faces scowling.

The beginner is a figure of contradiction, conditions what has begun.

Someone could say clouds suddenly, correctly, there's a change in the low-lying blue, the space for it having diminished, its limits are almost certainly black.

Yes, black is right, it's for certainty, yellow for cattle, brown for the violin, pink is fortuitous except in flowers especially the rose, rose is for the rose, gray for clocks and the time they keep, orange for lips or for cups, also sponges, ochre for shadows at noon and sleep, silver for fish and memory, fissures and their accompanying sentiment, gold for blue and iconography and geographical distance, red is for the forest and for the alphabet, blue is for intelligence, purple for the old neighbors smelling of wool, green is for sweat, and out of white comes what we can say.

The face is made from paste and paper, this is what's known as clay, the skull is formed of clay supported by feeling twigs into which feeling flows.

Some degree of risk is involved, but no one pities the beginner.

How can they until he or she has begun (to be pitiable or enviable, happy or sad (one can't experience happiness without catching a glimpse of life (February 1) since that's what happiness is: the awareness of the sensation of having seen something of life), rich or poor (money is both signifier and signified, and poverty is like the notorious gap between them (February 5)), well or ill (inevitably in the course of time one will be both, though for some wellness is the norm and illness the marked condition (for these people illness is an injury) while for others it's the other way around (illness befalling the ill is an insult)), etc.).

And then it's too late for pity.

If in the 19th century, as Gertrude Stein said, people saw parts and tried to assemble them into wholes, while in the 20th century people envisioned wholes and then sought parts appropriate to them, will the 21st century carry out a dissemination of wholes into all parts and thus finish what the 19th century began (February 7)?

Even when nothing happens there is always waiting submerged in the task of beginning and task it is in thoughts to begin afresh.

The beginner makes a beginning, and if optimism is in the air (or pessimism, that mordant state of mind that says things can't possibly improve), the beginner proclaims it a good place to begin.

That is beginning.

Something and other things in a sequence simultaneously.

Ants on a white sill buried.

A harbinger in the light.

A child composed nudely.

A side of tree cut into squares at a shout from a man under an umbrella.

A furtive marked moth fluttering into a beam of light.

A woman at a door falling.

The beginner is diverted.

Follow me.

Beginning will be an experience, unfolding more it runs its course, we will follow, doing and undergoing.

We have no particular end or plan.

We could head out, in, off, over, north, we are doing so.

Which?

The answer must be deferred just as I write this, a child comes into the room with a book always a little differently, he says, I don't like gloom, so much the better, I say.

Something is happening.

To the book?

Yes, to me.

The child is holding a spider on his palm, perhaps he'll be very strong, minds will fly to meet his, I'd say thinking, hello, what can I teach the flesh about his body, the snow, cake, time, without question nothing is more amazing than the millions of years.

The spider jumps off his hand, whoops, no calculation, the transition is sudden and remains elusive, there is a spider and then it takes power with a "tightening of the heart strings," it takes itself off.

A beginner (a tragic as well as a comic beginner) must have a sense of timing, though perhaps not of time, which can come only later, as lateness, animals too, cats, zebra, frogs, etc., they must know whether the time is wrong or right, that is timing, whether the given moment will be a passage into or out of disturbance.

Whether we lie in a field or sit in a small room, we know we are living in an expanding universe (March 19), there is mathematical uncertainty and certainty about it, F = freedom, there's an echo, mockery, perhaps.

I've begun without stopping maybe lurching and poorly fitting.

There's no heroism involved, heroics come to a stop.

The snapping of whistles, rumpling of twigs, spinning of bricks into bridges goes on in confusion trivialities cross.

You think of confusion as rapid?

As it proceeds at a turtle's pace by halves?

Coming or going?

One can't tell.

The turtle halves in motion, etc., as et cetera in celebration—we don't know wholes (heroes (March 21)).

I can believably anticipate breezes in weather, memory, precision, noises of birds or perhaps cellos or both alternating, some by day some by night with its stars, cravings, evaluations, distractions, goals, and fumblings where there are no goals, since beginning is undertaken but not always with the goal of beginning nor with any goal at all.

I would never want to suggest that one begins by oneself and not in conjunction with one's own life and with all the rest of life besides, with its conflicting tendencies.

That would be a mistake, not an impossibility, mistakes do happen.

Still one may begin unawares or one may be well on one's way but feel it perpetually to be a beginner's way, one might insist on that, an old hand at beginning and getting to an edge for the love of it.

Hesiod says love is a loosener of limbs.

But it is fate that has given the spider freedom and it runs for cover, it doesn't exhaust its possibilities.

Angered at my rapidity, my strength as I release things and lose them, I have to push the beginning back.

Back from grieving yet to come, happiness coming, obligations as hard as iron, curiosity swaddled, given.

I am about to experience something, it is already underway, I began to experience it several nights ago, that was guesswork.

Something is launched, yes, the music is beginning, is beginning beginning, is. . . .

Brightly flashing, history is made.

I knew that before I thought it entering the room (to become a site of remembrance) in which I didn't have to be very old to know what the chairs were for, why they were there—to know that was beginning.

Listening, especially at dawn, to birds, seductive facts, we listen to their songs as to the song of brains.

We wake and dream wanting a great accumulation of adventures, as complex a thought as possible and all there, if only for a minute, nothing but passage.

What things know no one knows, what we were we don't remember, nothing stops, clarification is constant and ubiquitous even if things are unclear and occasions don't endure.

Unable to remember, the beginner guesses.

The beginner wants a raison d'etre so that beginning won't seem pointless but the beginner has to begin before a raison d'etre can appear.

The beginner is what becomes.

Morning occurs after daybreak has begun, the beginner faces, parries, closes, proceeds, all having begun, it's the substance of his or her speculation and ignorance.

I know what time is, I'm ready to write, but I can't define waking (March 23) when night falls sleeping when animals are led into the fields.

Indications are not enough, indications with obedience to provide information beginning to do the job even before the small divisions are accurate enough though never accurate enough to discover the beginning.

Just out of reach of the beginner in bed stand the wheels, they count teeth.

Water from the water bucket falls, this means escapes.

You'll remember the time the patterns were frozen at the beach all at once but inconsequentially, you'll remember feeling like a "freak" yourself, you'll remember is something that can be said to a beginner.

You'll remember when someone resembling N, it may have been she, stumbled bashfully and discovered a fragment of a dinner plate, a pearl, and an egg.

When from four spaces sound filled apparent thoughts.

When the dismantled split-second after sufficient chipping was ridged so that something could be said of it.

You will.

Early on a given day, one noted but soon lost in a sequence of days, each becoming indistinct except as part of a "period," it being easier, it seems, when it comes to time to understand a sequence (of days, weeks, months, or years) than any single member of it, periods being false ends, as much for a past master as for a complete beginner, a blind baby on its first day, N or G appears, at first some distance away in the light and wind but from the start rapidly approaching, the distance being halved in no time and halved again in half of that, until who it is can be distinguished, a woman reading a book, then it would be N turning pages, but approaching what or whom?

What is the zero point, where and whose is it?

In "X" Barrett Watten says, "Start anywhere."

Ferociously one must drive on to tenderness.

Barrett Watten continues: "Alarms. Concentric ring."

This conveys the experience of beginning to see what one begins to see and with that knowing has begun.

To the beginner knowing arrives unknown and uninvited, not intended but neither fated, it is not just spun sparkling to be spread into patterns or wizened to a point for a time he or she will want to revise so as to make the knowledge useful.

But now long past beginning—or, rather, as a longterm beginner —I can ask.

What is it?

Pitch?

Collision?

Instrument?

Or perhaps sting, history, perhaps time, perhaps morning or death-to-come of which there's no knowing?

Which?

Yes?

It involves a long series.

Lip, dust, factory, watch, window, work comes in.

We live between walls.

We inhabit conditions we term chance, sequence, and agency, this is a place where things happen, we can say "on that date things."

To say so is to create the conditions required for beginning.

But in the middle of doing so, I am caught watching myself, I am past beginning, my foot is in a red sock.

On the wall is a wedding photo.

Do the walls need our tenderness?

The familiar are guests to the beginner.

As passengers out in or of the blue we come to things, I don't mean metaphorically, for example, as passengers, there are already plenty of transit metaphors, but from the beginning (a point preceding the metaphorical) and in reality even in our absence (unless the beginning itself is metaphorical, I think it is, surely it is allegorical).

Absence, of course, is allegorical, establishing an allegorical presence (March 26), we arrive at it through affinity (but a beginner has affinity with absence to come since beginning creates a demand for presence) or through sense perception ("there's something to this," "that's in the way," even "that's it in the way," etc.).

To define the beginning position as that of the egg is to leave the beginner in the nest of fate.

Deserting that nest like a child the beginner enters the world as a newcomer, a stranger to the world, where he or she may be at a loss—a child who, having lost his or her adulthood, is in search of it.

To the beginner the world is its beginning, but the world to the child is in ruins, the child feels miserable, sulks.

It really is melancholy being a beginner.

Nonetheless, except when it comes to food, children enjoy more things as children than they will as adults (whom the child while taking charge will regret becoming when becoming an adult).

One stroke and it's done, says the woman shaking her fork, and because of the similarity between one stroke and beginning the beginner feels that what's been begun is done.

Desertion is impossible.

Do you remember how I clung mournfully to the threshold when you played the violin? the beginner asks.

Almost all children have preternatural skills and a highly developed aesthetic sense.

Out of that their sense of time emerges to grant them the possibility of a sequence, a sentence, the point and period of which are yet to be discovered, yet perhaps to be determined (we can state that the moment is now (April 3)), towers are created while crumbling occurs on its own.

Children tumble heroically, they arrange events so that they can tumble afresh in soft bushes, unpunctuated plaster, failing light, embers.

They bend, the hour is bound somewhere.

Time matters to experts but it is everything to beginners, who don't want to get up in the dark unnecessarily any more than anyone else but who don't want to be left in the dark either, they don't want to miss out on life, hardly anyone does, though I'm not such a beginner myself as to deny that some do, some come to that, to wanting to be left in the dark, that is, yes.

One "comes in from the dark," that's the phrase we use, the room (a room just like the one in the book in which it will later be described) metonymically representing the realm of perceptibility, plenitude, and light, the dark representing the void, the casting of things into invisibility and hence into imperceptibility, into absence, and out of experience, yet to begin.

"I," in cease continuing, weigh without erasing.

"I" in piracy on a porch, a pilot coming through the dark over a city, hide from war.

"I" in my own idea of what must be inevitably never preclude outbursts.

It's not I doing it all, the buttering and alphabetizing.

It's impossible to collate all the changes of mind that bring us things hard to catalogue.

Things we can't change—specific dreams or deaths, griefs, gifts drawing close—we can't edge.

Can we hesitate?

It takes more than seeing a piebald horse browsing beside a murky pond and more than being Anna Karenina to figure out what and what besides.

It takes observing for example, but the example itself will surely change.

It takes leaning a long bicycle against a smudged wall and stumbling over a bent bicycle beside a sucking ditch to distinguish between against and beside.

It takes arguing with a person against an idea and declaring that one is bound for the hills and experiencing a sensation of momentum beyond all expectation and declaring this a sky beside which nothing is more blue to distinguish between against and for and beyond and beside, which is to say there's no end to it, which is to say we're getting to it now.

There's an infinite connection to perform.

No stop.

We subtract, loop, erase, rope, return to zero, tug, and begin over again.

Things give way, then things assert.

They appear in photographs.

"When I was 14 I went to Spain.

"One early morning in Seville I left the hotel (of which I remember nothing but deep gloom) and walked into the exhilarating but devastating sunlight that seemed to hover, to cascade, to penetrate like some philosophical quandary.

"Could fate exist without us?

"No matter the answer, I was frightened.

"I saw a small donkey; though it was trotting toward me—because I was sad—it was absolutely still" is such a photograph.

But now the things in it have given way, yielding to different assertions.

Like other beginners, the child makes an array of connections between a large number of people.

I don't mean that they happen around the child, I'm saying that the child makes them.

Later she forgets this, but that's the substance of childhood.

A foreshortening, it's really a form of freedom, it seems so inevitable, so normal, that no one imagines it could have been intended, but in what direction does it go?

What is shortness, what shorter?

Sorted? thought?

Size is derived.

To see a size, particularly one that is very large or very small—it is like looking at reality, size is so full of life.

No matter how much one prepares, one must take jumps, and I don't know what, because they are so active, to call them unless playful (dramatic) and promising (even more dramatic).

But why jump?

Well for the most part (May 7) it has very little or even nothing to do with whence or whither one jumps, one jumps to jump, then? yes, one is impelled, one jumps as one blushes, sneezes, weeps, smiles, dodges, keeps time to music, all in response to ordinary but special excitements or sometimes to none at all or in keeping with one's mortality, but with respect to that there's either keeping (in, for example, the shade of a tree from which one can imagine oneself walking out into the sunlight) or jumping, one has a choice, a chance, that's fate: the arrival, the finish.

Very slowly the aching Odysseus leaps homeward (so the novel might begin) but home takes alarm—it arranges itself so that it seems to consist of nothing but the place to which memories fly and from which yearnings depart (Penelope waits—as for her weaving, who could ever analyze it?).

There's no end to the thread, as Emerson says, "the bird hastens to lay her egg, the egg hastens to be a bird."

13   SUSAN HOWE

from Bed Hangings

Revisionist work in

historic interiors spread

from House to Museum

Other documentary evidence

Friends who wish to

remain anonymous

Contest between two
singers *Conflictus ovis
et lini* if the heart or
eye were cause of sin
Rival claims Summer
Winter Soul Body Wine
Water Phillis Flora

Ordered wigs cloaks
breeches hoods gowns
rings jewels necklaces
to be brought together

Go to—my savage pattern

on surface material the line

in ink if you have curtains

and a New English Dictionary

there is nothing to justify a

claim for linen except a late

quotation knap warp is flax

Fathom we without cannot

A small swatch bluish-green

woolen slight grain in the

weft watered and figured

right fustian should hold

altogether warp and woof

Is the cloven rock misled

Does morning lie what prize

What pine tree wildeyed boy

Counterforce bring me wild hope

non-connection is itself distinct

connection numerous surviving

fair trees wrought with a needle

the merest decorative suggestion

in what appears to be sheer white

muslin a tree fair hunted Daphne

Thinking is willing you are wild

to the weave not to material itself

Ten thousandth truth

Ten thousandth impulse

Do not mince matter

as if tumbling were apt

parable preached in

hedge-sparrow gospel

For the lily welcomes

Owl! art thou mad?

Why dost thou twit me

with foreknowledge

To this the Nihtegale

gave answer that twig

of thine thou shouldst

sing another tune Owl

Still in Ovid cloth of

scarlet the Owl and her

"Old Side" blue thread

Listen! Let me speak!

the Wren replied I do

not want lawlessness

Everyone knows in a rough way

the impious history of sensation

Earlier times resemble ice to the

fourth parish or enthusiast class

Sheets and pillows are initiated

Permanent thought permanent

Before inviolate love knots are

edged with paper in the manner

of braided binding valences before

a long night's sleep with closure

Evening for the Owl

spoke wisely and well

willing to suffer them

and come flying night

from the Carolingian

mid owl falcon fable

In their company saw

all things clearly wel

Unfele I could not do

Nihtegale to the taunt

Owl a preost be piping

Overgo al spoke iseon

sede warme inome nv

stille one bare worde

Go he started mid ivi

Grene al never ne nede

Song long ago al so

sumere chorless awey

Milk they drink and also whey they

know not otherwise bitter accent

I do not remember any crying out

falling down or fainting to signify

revelation preached from Isaiah 60

I have not known visions trances

Who are they that fly as a cloud as

doves to their windows have pity

From terrible and deep conviction

Brandish unreconciled yet arrow

Pensive itinerants and exhorters

gathering manna in the morning

Thirty pages then the rest mostly

children enact ruin enthusiastical

impressions in my mind though

not to my knowledge it seems he

still believed he was conversing

with an invisible spirit however

the sharp weather his wet jacket

Finding himself alive went home

Something over against Mr. Sprout

He can be found in the cool

of evening rolling in his

chaise with his shepherdess

Wearing a large Presbyterian

cloak somewhat soiled with

a full bestowed wig a month

or six weeks diligence will

teach him the exercise of

the windpipe

Some prepared cloth or other
left simply in the hair "glazed"
or "lustred" a kind of twilled
lasting when stouter John Legg
of Boston left to his daughter
1 Coach bed camblet curtanot
vallens to disenchant blessing
All lands and to the bordering

Malachy Postlehwayt (ed. 1773)

defines Calamanco as "a woolen

stuff manufactured in Brabant

in Flanders" checquered in warp

wherein the warp is mixed with

silk or with goat's hair diversely

wrought yet some are quite plain

When did appearance ever justify

It is requested that those who
discover errors in this work
not mentioned in the ERRATA
should give inforrnation of them
to Mr. William L. Kingsley of
New Haven and if it seems
desirable they will be given to
the public together with other
facts and statistics ADDENDA
The great Disposer of events
is exchanging what was good
for what is better history that
is written will be accomplished

14 LISA JARNOT

Brooklyn Anchorage

and at noon I will fall in love
and nothing will have meaning
except for the brownness of
the sky, and tradition, and water
and in the water off the railway
in New Haven all the lights
go on across the sun, and for
millenia those who kiss fall into
hospitals, riding trains, wearing
black shoes, pursued by those
they love, the Chinese in the armies
with the shiny sound of Johnny Cash,
and in my plan to be myself
I became someone else with
soft lips and a secret life,
and I left, from an airport,
in tradition of the water
on the plains, until the train
started moving and yesterday
it seemed true that suddenly
inside of the newspaper
there was a powerline and
my heart stopped, and everything
leaned down from the sky to kill me
and now the cattails sing.

What In Fire Did I, Firelover, Starter of Fires, Love?

The glow of it in early winter, the barn that Eric Bartlett and
Ronnie Burke burned down on Sturgeon Point Road in 1981 and
not on purpose, the coils of voluminous smoking snake pellets
set off in the driveway and on the porch steps with the neigh-
bors' kids, the activity of Jim in finding the biggest log outside
the house to put into the fire, the burning things upon the
beach—paper cups, straws, tires, and also driftwood, the build-
ing of all such things to a cone of six feet high on or near the
night of the fourth of july, annually, the specific red candle
flame in the kitchen at two a.m. in 1987 having consumed a
mushroom stem and cap and after having returned from the
supermarket neon, the silver lighter Peter gave me in 1991 that I
subsequently lost when I lived in the back room off the kitchen
in a house on Ashland Avenue, the napalm that we made with
styrofoam and gasoline and flung from slingshots onto moving
cars while burning, the brownish edge of plant leaves in the
middle of the living room beneath the sky light, equadistance
between the two giant fish tanks in the place in Oakland by the
phone without an ashtray, the bucket thing of ashes outside
Kevin's bedroom window, the clicker for the gas stove with the
broken hook that couldn't hang upon the wall, its reflectiveness
in midday so as to be nearly invisible, the imagined heat of the
outer planets and all burning that there is, the oppositeness of it
to appliances known as fridge, the barbeque we never had in
Brooklyn cuz the charcoal was no good, the comet that we saw
from the same porch with the barbeque which was a fire in the
sky, the supposed end of the world, the subterranean lakes of
fire, the song called Ring of Fire, the words firecracker, firedog,
and firehose, the fire in the fennel stalk and also then
Prometheus, all general ideas of warmth and glowingness, the
variety of foods that can be cooked with it, the use of it to see
when there's no electricity, its ability to melt wax, the way it
starts from broken glass reflections, the way it melts sand into
useful glass, the way it can be used to shape things into glass-
shaped swans and also other birds.

The Specific Incendiaries of Springtime

Inside of my inspection house there are
things I am inside of lacking only linens
and the tiniest of birds, there are small ideas
of tiny birds and things they are inside of,
in the middle of the small ideas of genius
we began inside of sundown,

I am hiding from relationships of springtime
in the tiny rooms with tiny birds, and there
are functions of relations, there are springtimes,
there are tiny birds and checkbooks and some
farmteams,

I am wanting only lemons where you have
wanted only linens in the center of the room,
I am waking up in long corroded rooms,
near Bakersfield and farmteams, in the vivid
dreams of rain, having dominion over these
animals and the salesmen on an island in
relationships with shepherd girls who carry
soft umbrellas,

Toward sundown, let me say that I am in
your absence forced to read a smallish book,
to read ideas of farmteams in the twilight
in the spring, where on an uninhabited
island I strangled all the shepherd girls and
then became a smallish book, and doused
the bed with kerosene he sleeps in doused
with birds and twilight books I dreamt of in
relations of the springtime that I dream,
Of farmteams, clearly let me say of sheep
and clearly let me say of spring in Bakersfield,
where I have strangled all the sheep and
several shepherds, where to read ideas
of twilight in a book, today, to a new love,

where in briefly retouched currency, functions
of inspections in the house now lacking lemons,
here I strangled all the shepherd girls and birds,
Where I read ideas of twilight to a newer love,
where the genius of liberty we began in the
middle toward sundown was a smallish bird
in spring outside of Bakersfield, where,
on an uninhabited island, to the twilight
of this genius in the book, to the mouthpiece of
the smallest sunlit bird, of the farmteam in
corroded blue relations, of ideas and in
inspection blocks, of occurring in the middle
of the twilight, of the dreams of smallest books
and salesmen inside Bakersfield, of wanting
only linens having wanted only wicker in
the center of the room,

I am a soldier of this wicker chair, I am
brandishing a welding torch and drill,
I am the island with the shepherds and the
sheep, I am waking up in Bakersfield in
rain, in a long corroded room, near the
farmteams in the vivid dreams of rain,
and in turning in the kerosene being slowly
doused in fire, I am, toward sunlight,
strangled by a shepherd girl, I am a salesman
of the islands of this currency,

Of rain, let the farmteams in relations
with the springtime in the checkbooks
find the rain, corroded I am, wanting only
lemons, only linens and then you, let me say
that you are on an island with umbrellas,
that we are woken in a room of springtime
birds, that nowhere is a smallish book,
and in the twilight reach dominions of our liberty.

Still Life

Where we finally move closer, but instead we don't move closer at all, we just have an understanding that we want to move closer, which is a form of moving closer, or at least something to think about, that it was an idea, moving closer, though not ultimately satisfying, though something, on one or two or three occasions, during a single night, moving closer, and the sands accumulate into sand paintings, that are colorblind, and filled with raccoons, and the steps of the sand toward the pyramid of sand are altered, wearing pumpkins on their heads, wishing to be loved, in the steps of the sand, terrified, or not terrified, moving closer, identifying with raccoons, on certain evenings, that maybe to go from there, because obviously, the sand and raccoons accumulate, taking years, listening to the traffic, saying is it quiet where you live, near the sand and the raccoons, in a quiet room, near the sounds of all the traffic that moves closer, on the periphery, that the thing is this, accumulating, getting closer, to the raccoons and the traffic that moves closer, having moved, having said that moving closer is ideal, having said thank you, and so forth, that the so forth is moving closer, forward, toward what in most of the universe would have been a scene, where the sand is forgotten, and the raccoons, and the accumulation of pyramids, and clothing items, and various identifications, and so forth, but instead, one by one, or one, or two or three times awkwardly, there is news, and there are raccoons, and the raccoons are screeching in the yard, as if to say something about the grains of sand, at opposite sides of the universe, screeching, with their suits and ties, bringing news, like Tom Brokaw, colorblind, reliable, and standing in the sand, and the news, which should not be true, but is, that there are raccoons, screeching, outside, in the traffic, near the sand, and on the news, and the curious figure that is him, there, who is reliable, and like the sand, accumulating, rightly, while how wrong it is, the news, that there is a rightness about him, the news of the raccoons, so close enough, and safely in the sand.

Valley of the Shadow of the Dogs

He could be so far outside himself, generating body heat, far
from the telephone, in a room, heated, with the outside of his
thoughts, turning, with precision, for the reasons he would
know, nearer to god and the mountains and the outside of the
room, with the chairs, perceived as objects, always slightly
passed, looming, on the forefront, like cake, looming, on the
forefront, ambitious, like a sumac leaf, lovely, a wing, with
wings and made of cake, having counted let me count, one, the
ways that there are, unused, potentially useful, held at a
distance like a flower filled with tiny bugs, loved and lovely,
without raccoons, beside the spiders, smashed on the sides of
the forks, lovely the form in the meadow of the shadows of the
dogs, howling, reckless, unusual, unfulfilled, with the christmas
lights, steady, and how close I am to myself, and how close they
are to the sumac leaves, lovely, against the rain, falling out, fully
heated, from the inside of his head, with spiders, in a meeting,
against the rain, given to this disposition, equally talented,
talkative, talking in tongues, beyond the heads of the cows,
friendly, on the staircase, friendly, where I waited and the city
moved, drenched beneath the sumac leaves, having fallen, into
the field, where the dogs are, looming, in the forefront, in the
shadow of the gods, dreaming of being alone, relieved, heated,
steady on the trees beside their wings, riding on the backs of all
the bears, and the bears, relieved to be the sumac leaves, and the
sumac leaves, relieved to be the bears, and the spider, on the
plate, relieved to be just so, wanting to be loved, where the city
moved, and then I moved, and the pins all moved, out of place,
tetanus-like, having syllables, wishing to love, wishing to love the
ocean and the ski runs and the sand, wishing to love the sheep,
converging, on the frontispiece, having thrown the ball, equally
having thrown the ball and having thrown it, into the leaves,
near the trees and all the dogs, meditating, on the coffee cups,
meditating, on the backs of all
the bears.

Poem Beginning with a Line by Frank Lima

And how terrific it is to write a radio poem
and how terrific it is to stand on the roof and
watch the stars go by and how terrific it is to be
misled inside a hallway, and how terrific it is
to be the hallway as it stands inside the house,
and how terrific it is, shaped like a telephone,
to be filled with scotch and stand out on the street,
and how terrific it is to see the stars inside the radios
and cows, and how terrific the cows are, crossing
at night, in their unjaundiced way and moving
through the moonlight, and how terrific the night is,
purveyer of the bells and distant planets, and how
terrific it is to write this poem as I sleep, to sleep
in distant planets in my mind and cross at night the
cows in hallways riding stars to radios at night, and
how terrific night you are, across the bridges, into
tunnels, into bars, and how terrific it is that you are
this too, the fields of planetary pull, terrific, living
on the Hudson, inside the months of spring, an
underwater crossing for the cows in dreams, terrific,
like the radios, the songs, the poem and the stars.

15 JOHN KINSELLA

Bluff Knoll Sublimity

for Tracy

1.

The dash to the peak anaesthetizes
you to the danger of slipping as the clouds
in their myriad guises wallow about
the summit. The rocks & ground-cover
footnotes to the sublime. The moods
of the mountain are not human
though pathetic fallacy is the surest
climber, always willing
to conquer the snake-breath
of the wind cutting over
the polished rockface,
needling its way through taut
vocal cords of scrub.

2.

It's the who you've left behind
that becomes the concern as distance
is vertical and therefore less inclined
to impress itself as separation; it's as if you're
just hovering in the patriarchy
of a mountain, surveying
the tourists—specks on the path
below. Weather shifts are part of this

and the cut of sun at lower altitudes
is as forgiving as the stripped
plains, refreshingly green at this time
of year. You have to climb it because it's
the highest peak in this flat state,
and the "you have to" is all you
can take with you as statement
against comfort and complacency:
it's the vulnerability that counts up here.

3.

You realize that going there to write a poem
is not going there at all, that it's simply
a matter of embellishment, adding
decorations like altitude,
validating a so so idea
with the nitty gritty of conquest.
Within the mountain another
body evolves—an alternate
centre of gravity holding
you close to its face.
From the peak you discover
that power is a thick, disorientating
cloud impaled by obsession, that
on seeing Mont Blanc—THE POEM—
and not Mont Blanc—THE MOUNTAIN—
the surrounding plains
with their finely etched topography
can be brought into focus.

Akbar

"I'm truly sorry man's dominion
Has broken Nature's social union…"
ROBERT BURNS

The swarming things swarm in the wall space as heavy
as liquid concrete the flawed wall fast collapses,
spilling out all is unclean in the bright sunlight
as they dash crazily into dusk, carcass on
seed so sown but wet seed and carcass as unclean
as geckoes hesitate over Leviticus
and then Samuel, guilt offering of five golden
tumours and five golden mice as the ark comes back
to solve the ills of plague, cantankerous sheep with
their stomachs bloated, the salt scars and the torn creeks,
the dozer on its rippled tracks cutting a new
road through the last stand of trees and the mice bursting
up out of paddocks and into silos and through
hessian and polyurethane sacks and into
houses—testing cupboards and children's beds, the cats
sick of the flesh of mice so satiated they
run scared from the seething blankets, the kids filling
holes with buckets of water and blasting ratshot,
crazy with buckets and lengths of polythene pipe,
every sheet of corrugated iron bubbling
like molten zinc, galvanised under the harsh white
moonlight, a collusion of seasons, the climate
just right, the parthenogenesis of brash top soil,
the tunnels the vessels carrying rich sustenance
to a shrivelling surface. As now ideas too
full for allotted space spill into the nervous
system like mercury, thought the stimulant to
a flurry of possibilities, a smiting
plague that eats away at the store of plump seed grain
collected from the fullest heads in the densest
crops on ground rich with nurturing—that no planning
or safeguards could prevent such a dark collusion

of seasons, of heat, of moisture, of a bumper
year it's avowed...but that's after the trap's been sprung!
So now the mice moving in their millions devour
with one mind, consuming the body of the earth,
squeezing through its pores, filling even space between
particles, until they become the one body,
the akbar of myth, the unclean creature that is
the flesh, the breath; that is the progeny of dirt.

The Rust Eclogues: Radnoti, Poetry, and the Strains of Appropriation

(1) AUTOECIOUS

the appropriation of a host
in the random dispersal
of words, hard investments
in the soft tissue
of national identity,
the singular mind is the passion
of heritage, the aspect of blood,
the notion hosting
the struggle, the call up
of the one body on which the soul
is parasite enough, as if there's
a need to talk with the words
you live off, their buzzing growth,
their singular obsession
with death as seasonally
significant
in this and more, as if you
couldn't say this is THE
auto da fé, as if accrued
love would be filed, "I" with this single
species shall examine need,
and as the host grows wizened
the spores make as if airborne
delivering yesterday's news
you are only living
through the communications
with a self that offloads
a myriad of voices
into autopilot, collecting
black box data
obsessively,
that internally
the dark cell

can't disappoint,
like dialogue
between soul and self
and the conceits
of biotechnology,
as if safe from an informing
segmented space,
as if no one looks in
on solitary, as all
surveyed remonstrate
with the instant view
of the multitudes: spores
anatomical, political,
well disciplined.

(II) HETEROECIOUS

Riven in the folds and clefts
like envy
it increasingly absorbs light
and wallows on moist days
harbouring tetanus
and rendering food crops
and collections of Hungarian
postage stamps
worthless, all hosts mutable
and fair game; its refrain
is soundless
and yet it reverberates
through all industry,
keeping the bastards honest
or sending them broke,
incorporating the oxidation
of nutrition and wealth, the symbols
of growth edging out the lustrous crop
as a fantastic collusion
of season and labour,

the lyrical eyes standing
linear and outside,
itself, no longer reliable
in the newly-made contexts,
become the compound adjective
in its manipulation
from past participle, like the gender
indiscretions of bread-making
from the very same nineteenth
century strain of wheat, maybe
from the fields of metaphor,
or cross-fertilized
in the language laboratory,
the leering investigative eyes
of the ag. department.
Sharecropping
as dross around the mouthpiece,
the seamy vigilante-ism of the press,
the glittering surfaces
defecting like layers
on layers of hate,
just being lesser degrees
of love in the conscription
of appropriate doctrines
to good feeling, the indulgences
they call appropriation,
the well feds of American
poetry, the wells where sound is absorbed
and yet rings in the water appear;
the reddish brown surface
discolouration
is the racism of words
as the weather hums
a few bars of a heritage
listing. Jealousy driving
the creative urge, poetry
the spiritualism of the material
religions. A few chips or flakes

in a test-tube, a glassine
envelope, the chart
in the sampler's hut,
the glamorous intrusions
of popular culture on old-ish
negatives, the consternations
of hyperspace outing random
associations of alliterative infestations,
the escape velocity, the mass of a star,
against poetry, which is like
an Elizabethan village showing
the old arts, no longer
cells watched over by
the commercially fetishized,
the contracted panopticon
is the lookout, and all is one,
and the profits roll if in the greater
stack the rust is diluted
and sold off before it can take hold,
consolidate, thicken, colonize,
procure, absorb, digest,
consume, render even the highest
quality product worthless. Ro-
tating the expansion
we contract the better half
like sharecropping,
documenting the common
identity, the self
of nationhood though some
of the we having cleaner hands
and bribing the sampler.
The stack is cleared
or dispersed beyond
the edges of the map, and that's that.
A new season, a stainless steel
multi-voiced and glamorous
factory. A spectacle!

Radnoti Quarantine: Razglednicas

The way those poems were more than familiar
with death, soaking fluid from the corpse, absorbing
the mud. Those postcards from the last suffocated
breath, as if composed deep in the ground, recalling
tableaux and movements of people on a closing
landscape, where just below the dark surface you lay,
feeling their last hesitant movements, their forced march.
Those mountains bringing God no closer—elements
of the sublime drowned in their own words, that you might
have said look now to the journey of the tiny
shepherdess as she moves with the ripples of cloud
over the small lake's surface, but send no postcards . . .
For I have read those you carefully wrote before
your last march, receiving them an age after they
were sent, long after you had set off—history
franking them with blood and mud. Now they have burrowed
into the rot of a collective conscience filled
with readings of war—that footage from Vietnam
where the officer shoots the VC in Saigon
straight through the head, the cameras rolling as blood
rolled onto the street and spread like a small dark lake
that would not be stilled . . . Fifty years later the same
traffic stumbles through the Balkans, and CNN
is there moving where it can while others quietly
tell themselves to just lie still. Purnell's History
of The Second World War I explored as a child,
with images of humans and pack animals
caught exposed on thrombotic arterial roads
that had finally burst, churned into the soil's rank
garden . . . When that road reared and whinnied like a horse
taut as guns thundered from out of Bulgaria . . .
Hesitating, I glance up towards an outcrop,
a heron splendidly awkward in its roosting
tree, hunched and primal over the dark swamp water:
poets aren't silent now, but the guns are behind
newspaper print, lurking in layer on layer

of tv and computer monitor screens, deaf
to their own presence like flocks of terrible birds
smothering the persistent voice of the heron
as it rises again and again, long after.

16 MICHELE LEGGOTT

thoroughfares await them

between city and heaven dear bird a coin

for eyes for the animal thrown onto the road

tattered drum dazzled cones *that we may abolish*

disaster the stars lean down inviolate aspects

and touch the world at twenty four points

to read its upturned face   *Heal with a star*

her eyes it said and loss spread out

a dozen blankets against the purple wind

but still we couldn't shake malfeasance   o bird

happy in fluent grass how will you make

the starry marches and silk of the sky

tumble yard by yard

into the lap of a woman spinning

thin dreams from perfect other places

dark torch

hey old flame   I swam

across the harbour just to buy you

some shoes   all night all night

in the water howling songs

uncontained publications of love

with a flea in its ear and its pants

on fire   fool! liar!

(waves arms) who am I to hold

a dark torch up to heaven

and the ferry's disappearing lights

I didn't have the boat fare

but I knew the fit of your feet

and the extraordinary hours kept

in that boutique   I swim aflame

the songs of good hope

I was bee-belly setting out from the island of the first morning,
banners streaming, delphic sons on hand. Four directions were
in my company, and the bowmen of Zenith and Nadir.
Everywhere we went I made songs to be fired into the hearts of
strangers. Gold dust and ivory were part of the return but mostly
the arrows brought back good fortune. Nothing more is needed
to prove us out of the world.

Then I lost the blue-flowered tree and learned bitterness and
not-bitterness though not in that order. The sky was full of trian-
gles and peacocks tumbling fish a water snake and a table moun-
tain. I was insensible and there were no songs, only fire-edged
letters scrolling off a silent face. My arrows flamed against the
abyss and were extinguished.

woodsmoke wintersweet winter-spring breakfast, a north-facing
balcony looking over the archipelago. One of the sugarloaves was
mine or a road by night across the southern ocean. East and west
I saw it again: far slopes of afternoon, lee shoulder against the
wind, atmospheric of the other's vision. All in silence.

It was gone and the chase boats useless though I knew where
to go and we were quick getting off. Coming back the water was
alive with seabirds hunting, feathers and fuss in a circle.
Whipped up deep. I slept again in the upstairs room and this
time the coast was clear. I am learning to walk in a circle.

omphalos

crossing quay crossing customs the end is here *that's it! no more! you can all go home!* M. Dumnov in a sandwich board shouting to ants on the Novotel wall the day government fell in the city of light. He was ignored. There were flags on every corner, bread and wine and lilies in broad cups, and plaques commemorating other sunny days at the top of the elevator well. The crowds surged after their boat. Doves flew over the city. Every step was a return without memory to a place of origin. *narcissi. baked chocolate.* Helium in the hands of children. Suds in the fountain.

There is a manner of people called Corybantes who believe when the moon is in eclipse that it is enchanted and therefore they beat their basins with thick strokes to release her. Their worship is performed with noisy and extravagant rites. They howl it out, dancing and glowing on the high tops with frantic fire. A procession is made and numinous images carried but the hour of conjunction is not revealed. It is said the celebrants sleep with their eyes open.

We went anonymous in the din, found students sitting on the ground with scripts beating their hands and saying nothing. In their eyes I saw the ring on my finger begin a clockwise turn. In their faces were our faces all dewy at the centre of the world.

17 TONY LOPEZ

In Memory

I missed it. So much did they make of this news,
Jean Tension and Steve Fray on *Terpsichordia*,
Precisely the tone we were looking for.
You hand over two month's salary for a word—
Here's one coming through now: Allen Ginsberg,
A cramped hotel room in the late sixties,

Black sticky opium. Nobody at home.
The numbers going sideways are train times—
"*Melancholia* has a plastic core." You know
It's funding that makes us aspirational:
External validation and review.
Where are you now Allen Ginsberg? Who is pumping

Your harmonium? Elgar Alien Pcoet?
We speed into the tunnel expressway
But can't read the graffiti, Allen Ginsberg,
Your senior conductor speaking. Formica Zen
Always being torn down and rebuilt, for what?
Not some future perfection: everyone does it.

"Anyone can write" you told John Drew. You, a man
Who cared to know what happened and made poetry
Without hope of any hope but what is constructed
Herein. Part-exchange on detached homes and yellow
Silence of three months. Who cares whether any of this
Is happening? Allen Ginsberg, you can do it!

You can find the brand name guru and holy ghost,
As we go past the gas works, a tongue in your ear.
Ribbons of scrubland by railway lines and razor wire—
A new lead on the free state. We have yet to make it,
Allen Ginsberg. I'm at Alexandra Palace.
What thoughts I have of you just now, what fantasies:

Of deluxe sentiment and men in tights,
With hiking boots and hanging baskets put forth,
An ivy-leafed geranium. Allen Ginsberg,
Faintest touch of lips on the big name
Of your generation. My heart skips a beat
At the speed-up through hypertext to real time.

What difference does it make if you're getting
The best head you ever had, Allen Ginsberg? Muggers
Snatch a few dollars but leave your manuscripts
So you go down on your knees in a bio-pic
We're currently developing. Imagine that:
Starving, Hysterical, Naked Productions plc,

The best minds of our generation. Can you
See it? Where is the expiry date printed
On these verses by Allen Ginsberg, Gent, BL?
Before Language: little black and white books
Passed round in school, real songs of insolence.
This is Bill speaking on thursday at nine, your time.

Allen Ginsberg, the very name is like a phone
Ringing in a train. And because you'll be awake,
The doctor will be able to talk to you throughout.
These faint echoes of Moloch, Sammy, patch me through:
Mohawk, Motown, Mohican, Motivator,
Who's fixing your juice in the hereafter?

Everyone's a little bit heterosexual,
Now that planning is making a come back
In the upright position. Allen Ginsberg,
The photograph reproduced on page seventeen,
Sometimes a curly shepherd lad, should be a
Vertical image, head down, facing pastures new.

Gordon's London Dry or *Tankueray* pink gin
Ought to be the drink we toast your memory in.
Were you able to raise that conference call
Allen Ginsberg? Are you rotting in Manhattan?
Or cast upon the Hudson river to fade away?
Where are those howling verses that used to be?

Allen Ginsberg, what peaches and penumbras!
What price bananas and sunflower sutras?
Singing a Blake song, chanting mescaline dreams!
Setting your poems in the supermarket
Of eternity! Re-inventing prophecy!
I'll see you later, Allen Ginsberg, wait for me.

Studies in Classic American Literature

Walking on the crusty surface, coming back
I heard a voice from way inside saying
"Start as you mean to go on" with calm authority.
Slack as any boy on hourly pay, let's wait and see,
To see what the pill boxes are for just here:
So many wires strung out over the land.
Whereas what I find immediately striking
Is the vibration of ill-fitting window trim,
The muted zip of foliage and cloud.
But the take-off gives the plane away and turns
All four propellers over gun slits in grey
Now frost-etched and crumbly, blind and dumb,
In fields that under high ridges are resplendent
In apple green / Autumn tints / snowy white.

Signs poke up among large dripping Friesian patches:
Wholesale electrical distributors, freehold for sale.
I pray with speed put on your woodland dress
We leave the boundaries and sweet gardens of home,
Virgil knew all about ethnic cleansing.
The ability to work with change is at a premium
A bottle of frizz-ease, the five-minute manager—
That phrase was meat from the butcher's slab.
Stand by, put your hands over your eyes, revise,
Think carefully about your statement. Could this be
A cereal ad, digitally remastered? Think big.
The product message, phrased in affirmatives,
Sprouts from wicket fences in quality time.
If you'd like to know more, please turn up your volume now.

Irish box, leather boats, seafaring monks,
The heavy swell lifts the ship and slams it down.
Molluscs that change sex because of boat paint.
Rum and black, mud in your eye, tarry old Jack
Star-gazy pie, stab you in the back, old crow
Old soak, old salty dog—breaking the surface
But keeping low, water halfway up the mask.
It's cold, dark, you see lights along the water's edge.
The ship leaves its wake on water and steams on:
It is impossible to explain the meaning of art.
Mist gathers, as if we're already far out to sea
Long after the quotas have gone, fish all fished out.
That is when a man is capable of being in uncertainties
Eliminating large areas of the original image.

I saw cables going down into the Atlantic
From a small sandy cove like a memory.
Lookouts at the windows with binoculars,
Maybe a radar scanner moving round on the roof.
The feel of this is early modern, menacing
And laden with myth: Rex Warner in old leather.
That the treasure of a nation is its equity.
Grainy blow-ups of lightning bolts on white walls,
Almost everyone in England writes poetry, imagine.
Wind rattling the windows, spray streams on glass,
Is there a way to test this recovered memory?
What is the point of all this stuff about fish?
Maurice Saatchi's hat, bonfire of the quangos.
The rosy bracts of bougainvillaea.

It's a psilocybin-cocaine mix called *Atlantic High*,
We have no current memory of those events.
Her binoculars were found to be full of sand,
A stash of electric-shock batons on the roof—
A menacing pause as they re-arm and re-group.
The back room is full of specialist rubber and leather,
We should remember Mrs Thatcher for "equity release."
Imagine all the people having enough to eat.
The special relationship made us truly great,
City blocks of broken glass, system collapse,
I had a lead on the False Memory Society.
Fish fingers pushed into knitted gloves
Better make pickles with unripe quangos
Bougainvillaea sounds like a great place to live.

They came like shadows through the Alleghenies
Reading *Pittsburgh Memoranda* (Sante Fe, 1935)
Bombed streets made a great playground for the kids.
I hear the Princess of Wales is reading *Moby Dick*.
The product wants development at this stage,
Needs characters: Berrigan, Peel-Off, Hell's Own Vendor—
How about the Robinson Jeffers Summer Surfing School?
It would have to be individual tuition I guess.
They say leading black Democrats want to release
Golf courses for building homes. Are there black golfers?
"Some circumstantial evidence is very strong,"
Thoreau said, "as when you find a trout in the milk."
Ronald and Nancy with their dog in leash-tow,
Moving, smiling and waving at the TV camera.

By pressing a piece of paper on top of the inky block
From Cape Cod to the Gulf, the fisheries gone.
He came to this estate to interview or witness
And has too many B2s already, no offence.
One of those shirts with a contrasting collar,
Old sweaty ash smell. A new business plan
With wooden sleds, rolled felt, ex-army torches
Clearing a war-zone in weeks. Rubble disposal.
The visit made a great and lasting impression
His style being formal, mechanical and flat,
For a whale ship was his Yale college and his Harvard.
He arrived and left in an ambulance, was locked
Into a loft with a coyote, newspapers, a walking stick.
It was always there, only now you look up, the sea.

If the skin is tougher than anticipated
We must apply more pressure; if it is thicker,
We maintain the pressure for a longer time.
Orange peel perhaps, or scars from leg irons:
I'm looking at performance indicators for performance art.
Writing on a continuous strip of paper which unrolls
Forging Pound's pre-Raphaelite *Cantos*, inventing
Chinese characters, neat planks, Helvetica type.
Just how did polenta become an alpine food?
They were pulled out of their cars and shot by the road
In front of the cameras, a half moon in the afternoon sky.
He was completely white, as if just dusted, bone and skin
Looking at the wasp going into the ground, down there,
Carrying the seed of a Eucalyptus to St Elizabeth's.

A small female passenger in a dark blue tracksuit
With embroidered fruits and flowers and Latin names,
White socks and moccasin style casual shoes
Nos patriam fugimus: a man in a cage
Being flown back from Italy to America.
One of those imprinted mammals in the nocturnal house:
Tired routines, a birth video onstage, performers
Intending, I believe, to drive out the audience
Who were too dull or too polite to move from their seats
At say £100 return. Snatches of Wagner
Lying in a bookshelf in anorexic trance—
Travelling once again in a time of great floods.
"Are you writing your memoirs?" the officer said.
Prunus avium, if I remember, criminally insane

And in sole charge of the American epic.
Early horizontal morning light strikes a deer
Looking back from a field at the train going by.
Black fingers push through housing project wire
In the city jail, some kind of hard-boiled scenario,
Without any irritable reaching after fact and reason.
Shells crash into the Presidential palace which burns
Orange and black. Another truckload of volunteers
Is going to reinforce the frontline against tanks.
Three prisoners recaptured on the Isle of Wight.
The production of beauty was never a more
Urgent necessity. Snow on marble (*Apuane*),
Some indication of the heights beyond:
Your name will not be revealed without your permission.

Dint

no such antagonism
serves to restore
a vested interest
in these fringe areas
a conventional surface
trying to expel
the tighter sense
between these barriers
for verification
and this mode of bathos
in historical time
slides into invention
a door to door salesman
refuses to relinquish
scientific knowledge
crossing the threshold
a recent *X-files*
the remainder of this paper
most ingenious theories
along the Hudson river
it is however
a surplus of frames
according to the rules
waiting for the bus
or incompleteness
we are our memories
I'll just skip a bit
contact zones
barely perceptible
traces of wit
and hostile attributes
at first appear
seeking to outrun
the turn of the century
more detailed accounts
of the agent's movements

between these figures
wishing to combine
a genial character
replaced an object
on flagging lettuces
in no way sincere
natural or man made
textual communications
to capture a person
in the absence of history
various rectangles
seem more equivocal
but a poetry groupie
can function on all
inherently different
this kind of emphasis
two equally provisional
ontological dangers
of internal repetition
altered by fractals
a throwaway soldier
arrives at the airport
since it concerns
a criss cross web
emphatically denied
an ordinary citizen
in the war of ideas
a crucial distinction
refuses to send
where ethical systems
a victim of gothic
jumps through the mirror
in order not to
on a tiny island
is able to combine
a split allegiance
probably the wall
legalistic and geographical

a flat repetition
more like a dream
to avenge my family
fractures and divides
a genre of dance music
never ceases to imply
rational sequences
crossing out the word
an analogous function
in misrecognition
I'll take a drink
pursued by ghosts
declining into factions
which the natives consider
a regional conflict
prohibido fumar
she imagined a sister
in 1943
I still can't see
their indelible mark
for different reasons
merely the translator
a stranger in England
the pseudo memory
parodies authority
where the masquerade
enhances this danger
implicitly recognising
the excluded middle
and so invites
a life of tension
didn't find favour
you are not supposed
in the summer afternoon
a voice that is absent
looking for an exit
you take off your watch
sufficient to fracture

the cold war era
seems to contain
a series of steps
made of dead limbs
ever was contented
to fill its capacity
and be shadowed by
madness and obscenity
poses like a father
to report the crime

18   Barry MacSweeney

Wreckage is the only Answer

Targeting me with your eyes, uplifted, two steps down,
you held me in your grip from that day one meeting.

Fierce lines about your face across the altar. Hidden looks.
Amazing Grace. Fiery duties drive me home. Plates, dishes.

I will love you awesomely always. That rim of cloud, black
upon your brow, is a signal of the worry inside your treasured
heart. Passion, ever passion, be my watchword so it is always
spring. Always passion printemps, primavera, silky sulky black
iris defined against the green and horny stamens pushed into air.

Those Normandy apples coming on the blossomed trees. White
as wedding dresses. Flakes of blossom gone, snow in springtime.
No lilies frou-frou, but perfect vice of nature, murderer of
blossom so we later can have apples. Will you pick them, child
loaded, before the sheep arrive? Be careful. You don't want to lose
the bairn.

The daisies are wonderfully pretty too, and the veins in the stems
reaching to heaven which is always spring. Sunyellow centres—sun
at midday heading west—and white, that white again, white as
chasubles at Christ Mass, Pentecost, Corpus Christi, September 23
when all is done.

For this year alone.

Seared to the echo

I wish I'd had a normal everyday life. Bacon and eggs
Tea for breakfast. Coffee sundays. Not gin and Co-op tonic before
the washing up. Just look at the complete attention Fernand Leger
paid to Les Disques, 1918. To me, that
IS NORMAL, Europe, Europe, Europe, everything's otherwise,
beans on toast, two bairns, two girls, or one of each and a wife
who loved me. There goes a secret, There goes a sonnet lost.
There goes a bonny daughter Beatrix Potter on her little mind.
There goes a sweetlipped wife with her face in the foreign window.
Animal. Fingerpointing. You're nothing more than an animal, beast
in the windrow, paws upon my face, too drunk to save the children
even if they were born and in this chillcoldhearth we had a fire.
Take my golden sunshine everlasting for all time wedding ring
And put it in the sty with the female pig you loved more than me.

The stunning stunned look I gave you, mother at the Sunday table,
was meant to freeze you on the spot. And it did, years after you
woke in darkest Northumbrian night and wept alone in total grief
just because I looked at you while placing wild-grown rosemary on
fresh-slewed Kentish country lamb laced with extra virgin olive oil,
I spoke to you even with my freshly-hardened stare, most hard
to make sure you knew I would never give you a wailing baby.

I wanted an ordinary life, mornings up, buses, to Preston, Bury,
Bolton, the Boneyard Club, then Bartok, Berio, Boulez, and sweet
meadows of England, the lay sun-dimmed fish in the deep ponds,
where we walked fresh-handed, rings clanging and clinging, before
the dire sunset of our days. They put their lips to your parboiled
Desiree quartet potatoes but never, never again would my lips
go close to yours as in a kiss from a wife to a husband. Ever
My words on the telephone were a contract between, a breakage
of the marriage bed and what we said in black and white. Never.

2

False alarms: you never loved Boulogne, Paris, the Tuileries,
those disturbed ferry landings towards the long, long beaches
before the harbour, where your hair was a glare in Normandy
sun, bright copper, henna on your shoulder-blades, red rust
when off came your white bra, the sleek waves rolled up against

our tremendously small apartment, beneath the cathedral, and
then you kept saying in your sleepiness: no children, not for you.
You knew then what I know now, You sussed the story early.

Yet on the dark well of the winding downwards stairs we gazed
mutually and hit the absolutely sudden mark. You looked up.
You said I love you. Two hours, It was that remarkably fast.

Almost we defined an age. Before your hair lost its sunset
redness to become natural ash-blonde, bleached and burned
by Kentish light, when all honeymoon trickery collapsed

into a funeral of misery. All the time we'd done a mimic.
What did we say then, beneath the deep-frozen ash tree bole?
Riddance came into It. And ridicule, curlew songs sung sharp

into the night laid flat on hay bales in vermouth of the piggery.
You stood taller than normal on the sill a torment in darkness.
Your still wild hair bloomed & stunned against the bourgeois paint.

How we lost the moment from our real real selves. And then
the door, left open as you drove away to the new bungalow,
across the fallen Spitfire marsh, where the best died for us.

The gold of fallen leaves sprayed from the car's magic tracks,
and you were gone out came the Famous Grouse and you
were gone for good, Pleadings died a terrible death right down

the telephone line. The ghosts of Dungeness smugglers haunted the soaking stairs. I let the snow inside, just to let you know I still believed in good weather. Far out, far gone, a ghost person, thiefess of my heart, feather in the night, no longer the market square lease, ferry gold card, goat's cheese. All driven back into the earth like nails like woe.

Totem Banking

for J. H. Prynne

The totemic fuse of non-events is rising like a fume
into a fakeless sky and then they are all disproved
by lapse into money greed and awesome self-possession
pathetic to the very bone fat and slavering with wilful want
I seek them not but hold a flinty anger here on the high ground
no fat felines in this house we are lean and run like proper whippets

All sludge is there with bonus prize money cash right in hand
it sloughs upon the tide and happy too as the wallets scrap it up
wrestling with begotten tongues to say it's mine it's mine it's mine!
how short of true possession grandly ridden of their ever sense
amusing I suppose from those who have never heard of Bartok
but also how disgusting and pathetic and barbaric and eternally
backward standing there reeling at the latest arts council party

whingeing in a will of creepdom in their total victim stance
may they lie forever all together in their poverty and blame

the exact stance of the universe is completely improper
dark and shining in the night perhaps a file for copper
used by Shelley or Bunsen burner where are we again
alone upon the brow reiving at the downside fierce pierce

where are we arrow that flash of fletchering into the dawn
airport what airport vast expanse is it what do you mean expense
there is an animal at loose in my heart what kind of animal
poetry and a hatred of the tamed animals poets have become

we often lie upon the dark shore beaten by the different tide
but never crush the opposition flash it into the lights feel yourself
not least the black ptarmigan as it wings its brilliant skywards way
towards grass-free Tarmac out on the Nenthead road how sweet
for slag to be delivered by tractor instead of straight wheelbarrow
by you with your broken hair and broken throat don't mention it dear

Otherwise the wastrel pot is there but will never exceed us
for together we are lean and against all stupid wastage fantastick
it seems in the night how brill there are many people and many
well that's fine sit down have a cuppa and a dry biscuit too
not to mention a dead leadmine way beyond the height of our brows

fizz fume the distant dance the electric trance
the nowhere brood strangled connections failed
correspondents largesse merchants house of Mammon
how hard the ground to stalk across wrapped with wimps
moaners fruitless no-ones yet still the Tarmac is gorgeous

crapping for a laugh in a country so diseased by pride & failure
under the allotments of heaven which nobody has noticed lately
for want of attention Punch and Judys all happy by the seaside
of their tideless lives what is that other word for jetteurs? Ah yes
to remember every avenue from the dim lights of Sacre Coeur
to Rue St Denis 1000 steps Laforgue nitrates washed down the pipes

ghastly importance peacocked around by strutting dwarfs
their time-frozen feathers lathered with crass shadows darkness
even they want so much without heading for it life on a raft
of brisking around the meniscus on a wing and a cheque book
rain so insistent flashing in worse than the collected works
of illegitimates everywhere as they treacle their supposedly upward

to scorched stars of yesterday homaging fromaging other failures
thank you Margaret who started this ill fire furred starred with greed
without moral combustion slack distasteful wallets extraordinaire
here we are then upon the gunmetal road without Pearl perle
rain sheeting down running now a river along the curve in the path

as we head for frontiers a handful almost not the ignorant or studied
by far between the blessed planets dearest you are there also
inventing many wondrous things and nothing nothing less than zero
can remove that from us not to name the names but we are there
applied to the advancement of history and all hoorays to that
and damn the rest to the banking system all false totems burned

I Looked Down on a Child Today

I looked down on a child today, not because he or she was smaller than
  me
or because I was being in my middle-aged way fatherless and
  condescending
but because he or she was dying or dead between the kerbstone and the
  wheel

I stepped down from the steps of a 39 bus today with sudden blood on
  my shoes
The lesions and lessons and the languorous long-winged stiff-winged
  fulmars
chalked against the sky and white against the unpainted lips of her

I looked down at a child today, Gallowgate, the bus was turning left
the child stepped out, leaving its mam's hand behind partly swept by the
  wind
and partly by blind wonderful enthusiasm for life we guard against
  increasingly

She stepped into the path of something she or he would never know
  forever
In an elegant but unassuming place where as a living they hanged
  prisoners for bread-theft
It was the eve of St Valentine's Day on the wild side of Geordieland

The white dresses were being collected from dry cleaners Darn Crook to
  Sidgate
the strategy of the masses was being unaddressed once more except
  through the tills
where paper receipts come clicking out increasingly slowly to everyone's
  annoyance

What a beautiful, brilliant day, tart with expectation of love and
  romance in Chinatown
or down the Bigg Market as lager casks were moved into station and the
  dance floors cleaned

I looked down at a child today, never having had one of my own,
    and having no kid

I can call mine in a very old fashioned romantic Barry
    MacSweeney Elvis Orbison Highway 61 way
O Robert it was almost where you left on the bus O Aaron O
    Dusty O Blackened Eyelids
I looked down upon a child today under the buswheels and
    knew whatever your name you would see

heaven and it would shine and be filled with pianos and
    trumpets and not be suppressed
and freedom would be written in moth-dust on every angel's
    wings
and there will be the music of Shostakovitch and Poulenc when
    you wanted to hear it

and the monumental poetry of MacDiarmid and Mahon and all
    spirits would gather there
and tell you when you awake again what lemonbalm was and
    you and say
I looked down on a child and bonnybairn in blood today the day
    before St Valentine's Day

Cute Petite

There is darkness in the house tonight, and the moon
cannot be seen. Clouds drag across the sky towards the west
all the way from my beloved cities and place. Quite soon
I will return there dreaming of Guillaume and Pierre breasts
upon my lips and hands collected in a right hand pocket driven
by the whip of creation until the raining dawn scampi and white
wine for breakfast 6 am watch the waves follow one on one riven
by dread of the future so buy a painting for £1,700 in a flight
of extravagance who cares you Faber kids always making cocoa
for the University of Boredom and strange deregulated muse
hey hey rock & poetry dumped by OUP must make you glow
with fantastic rage how glad I am if I may be a real-life fuse
to destroy your plastic reputations. I will talk against you
each chance I get. Deregulator, new establishment, absolutely true.

19 ANNA MENDELSSOHN

The wrong room

Make no demands of those you are about to sacrifice to the winds
the white plume burnt in white fire, sacrifices, pressed space
spare no devastating word, the lambs were safe, your curse travelled
having infected my ears with the sound of your hatred
it was a word I did not want to hear. Must you hate?
Must you change every girl into a president, into a politique?

The sun never submits itself to the moon's phases.
Of light there is no higher tune. Everywhere enquiries flee.

Strictly personal

indirectly kind fire is glowing over forgotten reasons,
could have asked for help, but the mother in me,
unborn & now denied all part apart from by those
whose love neither sought me nor was by me sought,
cared to keep couples together with their children
rather than present my named self to endanger
their peace when in a sudden dreamless world
of no true life I was thrown as though I am a dice
who needs no table and no life to say no to.
no-one hears me when I speak, it is not total fiction.
They know everything about me I won't simply
take these words, I see, it was a simplification,
and now there is no need, and I have nothing.
What would my line have sounded like? an ascent?
a descant. but the door had been slammed
and Wordsworth had dried up over stones
on the edges of a desert where the sun beats
mercilessly since Berlin had been overrun &
beauty in the desert it was to become
the latter light of what had come to be
called irrational, that is civilization,
that is civility. I was further along the road
to death. and my arm does not present a
right direct or my waist go straight to death.
For how far from the city named was I pulling
my mind for a truer colour, clear of the acidic
red that has come through nature's wit to grow
and singing a reply, writhe immobilized.

Britain 1967

you draw me skating on the sky through a black mirror
and afraid of your country that it means something
has given the earth a pain whereas the clover clubs
whereas letters unconscious of toes on the lawn,
the wall, iron, waiting for the entrance to the world.
whereas you invite me to dine, or as you write; to dinner.
& the strawberries were the rent and the slippers
unmarked on the end paper. I was not loud enough.
Europe was educating me in controversy. never arrives.
wives weep   Europe never arrives. & the decoy hides.
you want to be known as a select committee—
who are the last to have achieved fine christ.
of myself diagonal, I have always had my reasons
not to reflect the moods of the times. have bellini.
I see that they are paid hounds working later on
Systems that have placed outside, total integration,
this is why, no answers complement eradication

On being reproached by saintly mediators for bad budgeting

I'd like to be rich. No not casually but positively streaming with wealth. Hard.
It is the only way to achieve anything. Nothing can be achieved without wealth.
To live in a great old house and never see the light of day, by which I mean
be exposed to public scrutiny. Never mind my accounts. I have no accounts.
Accountants are stupid little racketeers who never stop snivelling. Two fingers
for the sound of a chord and the end of a day when sin becomes annealed
to accountancy. Drinking a hot mug of coal. King Dick II down the mineshaft

Snivelling soap sud professors frothing pacifism as though anyone had told
them not to. The bromide feminists raking french knits off the shelves
who are these people who climb into vats of lye with years of police work
behind them. L'essaim. La foule. L'étranglées.

Franked

Lines from terrain are attractive trilling & deeply rolling theodolite
doing crash on the tiller. sceptic. disclos. the story of unlocked wrists,
magnetic fields etched by guidance with a brain being knotted,
in eyelash corners slashed. holding the reins, unstreamlined
pregnancy baited by quotient rushes slowly, too slowly
for strapped to a garland. a desk has a language complete
this is not, though, a language of love but of ovens & covenant
glimmering harbours where forgotten and dismal houses
shudder in heat throwing miasmas over interludes

～

held by compulsion untremored, glancing over jigsaw
looked over one arm timing its sweep to extremity
raw legs from the ankle down approached with caution
known for their less than round toes, unfortunately
there was something to be said, the invader did natives
a favour, aesthetically, by introducing rounder toes
to remove myself, the narrow gate of democracy requires a line
that has not mistaken misfortune for sublime purity
not Intrusion but Innocence destroyed by bad translation

～

quotient over. I totally disagree. Visconti escaped the firing squad.
Unfortunately to be born & then have to go all the way back
to be unborn, although alive, is an inducement to illusion.
I only want two words Unfortunately and Although, we have a sense
that was intruded upon by a look and a resonant note
I shall not be signing, from territory which I did not seek.
Not after those pretensions to knowledge. Even though I looked young
and my voice ceased to survive insidious recognition.
I shall not be signing. Only beneath the table, is the stage.

Photrum

deeply enclaved gnon spirited away from araldite,
no artists named in texts, appreciations appear laterally;
sorry. it was unacceptable to me to switch the muse of peace
for the muses of war, exactly how ranks are built . . .
nominalism is an imposition on sympatico poetry
there were no words, apart from a rehearsed disapproval . . .
that's O.K. we have boyfriends, we don't settle down
to cosy conversations with the opposition
who follow us from town to town with sexual innuendo.
I am not angry. I had an education in comradeship.
so that I have always had a lot of time. but not for filth
or smuts shoving line after line into windblocks.
I must say—that I am glad that my parents did not
work for the police force. I wonder—whether
rinsed keys mark June, i.e. defying unpreposs open debut
frein, do you think that drivers make better pianists?
well loan me your limousine for a spin by the coast road
there's a copse, or a spinney, with a hell on its hilt
papers are birthrights, spilt by content, emasculated intellect
carelessly codifying sisters for foreigners, cultural bolt
seats imaginary cuneiform arched steel bough
a pristine Harry Watt's film, incensed by human inability
frein take seven, heavenly word, a joke, good play, 'The Malcontent'.
Secular nebulous realism. Uncover yourself Psych. Flip off.
Idiots wear poems to read themselves. and are backed.

footsteps climb whereas they descend

I)

footsteps climb whereas they descend
lightly weeping mary rustle of paper
why they should play spoons
and rise again the footsteps
steps on trays
wrenches out of porcelain
after glass sheeted mountain houses
time pictorializes gas lamps
appoints peripheral imprisonment
paper birds inaugurate a child's conversation

II)

darkness falls fast
that there is laughter
leaving complete separation
far from Greek
unreceptive to Spain
constant electrical pulses
centrally receding

downhill a red beam
from the Constitutionnel
arriving exactly where the darkness
fails between days
to distinguish the hours

III)

seven Friday, was it free
what is free cannot be stolen
what I make without limbs
bends to break its neck
although not quite five
weeping mary the forest fire
at sunset wanting to go
no. July is blue.
the circus is hung in sports
bloodsuckers lunge at my vein
trying to find the prison in my blood
to feed off its nature,
which is nothing apart from memory
starved of movement.
which is played against a new book
announcing a Jewless space,
a Judge, and a Saviour.

20 ROD MENGHAM

Names in the Bark

The dog in his day is born and
runs out behind the palisades

assigned by his mother to light removals

running amok and cutting down on
essential vitamins. Some people are like that imbibing

and emitting sounds. Changing the odds
they go round in pairs a minimum of two

must live apart. Surround them with vectored cash
and false credentials. Don't even try to shuffle the pack
with clean hands. Today you were

catching your breath in the Temple of Victory

when the cries came from outside
products of more than one language

it was the Isle of Dogs. No such place
and no dream pays its way.
We have been stung feeding the plants

with grade A poison. There is the hornbeam
whose circumference does not add up

to the arrogance of a royal pardon
it grows in the field regardless

allow time for leaves to drop.

To the Soviet Embalmers

This one cartouche surrenders
the famous curse. Nil advice

on sharing the tasks
preparing the ground and pruning.

Pick-your-own name as a performance
I am out of touch with

mortal illness. The memory skids to
her box of tricks right there
in the Attic vase. Numerous other

sole agents set up their stalls:

impassioned choughs and
counterfeit magpies

drink from the well before the assembly
detour ends. You magnify the quandary
and its whispering roots;

for the martyr nailed to local colours
unable to utilize the construct

is just outside the rocket stadium
in the strong toils of reverse thrust.

Smitten

Before dawn all the first born
died under the anaesthetic.

Paper, ink, pen and all
the poisonous skin is heir to

started to feel utterly strange
I still have the ticket

lights go out and this automatically
puts hope into the hygienist.

They named a clinic in Chicago
I have never walked into

in the dark of the stem
although hidden now is the balance of power

the square root on which life depends
but that's not the only answer.

The casual tourniquet has ceased to turn
I explain to the children my nightmare

hating the mainland as it slips from view
for the breaking surf has covered it over

with everlasting moisturiser.

Another Name for the Cassiterides

In the glare the gannets dive
slanting their reports, like Pliny

brooding over asterisks in the original
Senate. Much more recent
royal shrouds recover from neglect
to wake up in another centrefold

of nature. One by one through fire and water

choirs of locusts setting out
in murmuring woodland dusk

between me and the audience battening
down the issue desks go home.

There is a tiny movement in
the broken boughs picked out

by Verey lights. The dunes make shift
terrifically in the Isles of Tin.

Allegory of Good Government

The moments of political yearning occur in the shopkeepers' vaults, where the gagged bystander is afforded a vision of the unaffordable. Fine deerskin boots hang just beyond reach, while the elegant chain gang of crop-haired maidens is wearing out its daily shoe leather. Its coiling dance repeats the braiding or weaving motion of civic prosperity, all too evident in bales of fabric spilling forward, decorated with cartoons of vermin, images of giant worms, flies and moths that latch onto the cloth their real-life counterparts would instantly begin devouring.

The brushwork centres on the circle of a tambour, a frame for embroidering violence. The absolute focus of two conspirators is only just captured and separated from the heart of the commercial district by this harmony through percussion. Unknowing, unseeing but all-suspecting, a single merchant sits cherishing his many wares. A procession files past, ignoring everything but its goal, round the corner in the next street, where the passage from single to married life is a gliding into the current. Alternating gradients of before and after, identical gestures, begging bowls no longer decorative.

Children bicker unnoticed, setting themselves up for careers of endless reprisals, covered in birdshit. The animal cages are empty, their hinges ungreased, while the artisan strays from his task of fashioning a body-double for the orator and fitting it with a wired jaw. Suddenly the click-click of gnashing teeth reaches the corners of the lecture hall. The orator stands with his back to the costermonger; siamese twins of motive whose livery has to be tacked into place.

Then the angels arrive by parachute, a defence against falling. A goatherd summons his flock, horns cocked, and drives them onto the landing strip. Sing me the burden of that song in which all the birds politely fake their expertise. Everyone prods the hindquarters of some beast or other; either that or, turning the goad on themselves, they try to guess in which hoof or pastern the thorn will appear, for want of which a hideous trampling ensues.

Earth tremors begin. The river stands still. A great slick of caviar collects on the surface. Builders swing from their trapeze, as tools and materials are showered on the streets. One late spring morning in Timisoara the roofs began to migrate. Heavy corrugated sheets flapping from one square to another, the whole town brought to its knees, because a spirit level is not the same as a watched pot.

Above the smog, construction is erratic; the whalebone scaffolds slip out of joint. With each wave of news bulletins, moonlighters add a storey to the creaking watch-tower, sliding the pots of geraniums around to keep it in balance. Townees head for the line of hills with battery chargers while drugged mowers enlarge their crop circles. A huge cloud of dust gathers on the highway. A distant hubbub. The charging contents of Noah's Ark, a three-lane relay in a Parthian shooting match.

Only certain walls rebuild themselves. Certain others topple further into the pit of Hob's End. Rent is demanded for piles of rubble, debt collectors stamp around with attacks of sneezing. Their demented clients are ashen on one side only, they turn the other cheek to police photographers. Flails and straw hats are reissued to the bomb squad, who outnumber the decommissioning board by three to one. As the crops die back the fatwah is discovered written in the fields. Birds of prey leave their solitary practices.

At this point, blisters erupt all over the projection screen. People avoid the bridges on both sides. Now the emblem of security is a hanged man whose blindfold has slipped; his calico pajamas billow in the freshening breeze, while the great scroll taken from its resting place fails to shiver and crumble at the lightest touch, scattering the fragments of its awful message. It can be rolled up into a militia baton and plied in the streets of East Timor. Noone sees the diaphanous safety catch or the subtle envelopes of restraint. They are more than likely to puncture your stomach if you get the harness tangled and pull the ripcord mistakenly.

On a narrow rock ledge high over the city a cadaverous wolf has been stranded, ferocity drained at last by the teething infants, foundlings that appeared in a dream, spectral and ravenous. The citizens are rehoused only after this period of complete abandonment to the savage guzzling of twins, moving together through selfish instinct. The ideal citizen is a twin; but a twin is always different enough and the founding myths are fratricidal.

The tiny figures standing at windows shrink from the light one after another; one by one they retreat from view and fade out, never to return, not even after the best efforts of government conservation spokesmen. Sentence after sentence, line after line, forever scrubbed bare.

Concession to Perpetuity No. 166

You can imagine the gestures appropriate to this tale of injury, of bruises given and taken during the headlong slide down shallow cliffs. When biting the kerb in a Paris street, there is no recompense, no handfuls of clay with which to sign the mould for your own passing bell. The master of a workshop with no assistants, preparing the ground for an alien vocation, rickety tools, zero patronage. That is the dream of recycling: a brightly suited council worker searching for rubbish in the tundra. Pheromones guide him along ancient tracks now covered by swamps and hummocks. Back at the depot, we are all posted as missing in action, after ritual exchanges of food and traditional dancing. Finely printed raffle tickets make the claim for a complex notoriety. Such is the display of legs.

Cats have always stalked the necropolis, sniffed the embalming fluid, known about decomposition through access to other frequencies. We sat in the snug at The Cardinal, debating the etymology of 'riot', a hound's following of the wrong scent. Even with the volume turned down, you cannot hear the feet of those running towards you until the last possible moment. They feed the desires of Pavlov: for whom lemmings were the ultimate challenge. What is it that causes you to bark? The burglar causes me to bark, that and the sheer pleasure of resounding, when the torches flare and the winds bluster. Yelping, snapping or growling in the conditional mood would impress me. Control exhalation, shake the tongue, wait for the larynx to drop; and don't come back until it has.

The dead men's coins are heads and tails, slightly uneven in weight, the right eye worth a full Ionian dollar, the left eye gone blind before the mast, staring at Caesar's image. The coffin encloses a series of lead stalagmites. The scalloping around the base signifies 'embalmed but conscious'. These hinges of the brain, these hooks (in the early models) of implication, have their false flings and tantrums, but they are part of the song. With barely a mouthful of rice between meetings, with his ear pressed to the office safe, he is rumoured to have gone for the 'Big Click', the barely audible passe partout of this glossary of insinuations.

After death, you go to an hotel, which hotel is called the Hotel de Nantes, where breakfast is not included. Close by is an architectural feature admired by the Surrealists, most especially by Robert Desnos (check this). An arcade without a project, a bow without a string, an issue without a body, a bone without hyperlinks. It is better to shop in a store that has been shopped in before. There are fewer cruel streaks in the fabric of this mirror unfit for the task of holding your breath. Your shoulders are in a different class, however.

21 DREW MILNE

from Bench Marks

Sweet shift go slow, go
amid shingle and roc
and be so the camera
lies in felt ice, in harm,
a brim too far, a maw
in litotes, our gorge
simply rises, comes to
to this general striking.

Or to some skurried bell,
sops a drift, democrats
in coup de main, row on
row and all for no one's
wedding, o dead rose
what murrain soldering
choler to fruits of gloom,
title tracks, this livid soil.

A cold comes in from
the links, sing of no
it will not do and then
is policy, from polder
to dry land, that's all
folks, now the labour is
in creels, gross lobster
to boil a living pink.

A scratch, a half moon,
pad on nail as you do,
out of sorts with party
hats, the heart eaten in
to marrow, o liquid
assets, dog days on the
verge, a bleeding marge,
a mount of crimson ease.

So go easy on the eye
above in fetid stars of
topic balm, high spirits
and cold accord of ruth,
sweet tigers, splash out,
your days melt in surds,
a fair and each to each
to the tune of millions.

The blue of the eyes is
never so clear as now,
in blind hands born to
bandage, plasters, each
map on vellum, a fringe
of sheperd moon, gone
to bleed, a braided spot
of bother so cancerous.

The taint of the carving
is in the slummy blood
of what grows feebler
in sulky grace, miasma
riding over, getting out
while the going is bad,
so less of that colossal
cheek & maiming sou.

Blue moon on fed day,
smiles so still, or soon
dies, drops a halo, hot
suits of nuclear electric
on th'ensanguined suns,
garb o grime, in rails of
bleached bondehede, no
ash of its worth or page.

O fucked city, its agon
lustre in foamy rind, to
do so soft with then on
acrylic afternoons, our
one good eye flowering
me with disaffections,
ah mine hurt, it shrinks
from less, it shrugs on.

So flower the baby for
pure boot and spur, to
list with zeal on banner
sky, each bright light is
you, for the taking, our
surfing oxide, treats of
burnished ore, its civil
song so shiney in wax.

Drop off of curtains
sleepless, so torn to
pale coats of acid lid,
the bends or spumes
up in optic fire, flesh
still pressed to trysts
of laburnum, arc of
our cuffs in poison.

Set freedom by storm,
livery shy, mope eyed
by living so long in
hab nab, whetstone or
mizzle, it's one to me,
death's arquebuse or
punch sore, but take
me for an open sword.

Bereft, put a cold front
in mood swings, curve
or cut legs to the quick,
scissile, at any rate, or
a goner, so sash keen,
scampy and hale, better
late ripe and bare than
blossom or umber blast.

Each to each, the braid
irks, fathomless in rank
peonage, chip in, drop
lustre, o barbed chaff,
your brim flows on as
feet go blow by blow,
stiller than a rude grant,
a cut price in demijour.

What a palaver, fond as
a drifting besom, fasces
and bengaline ripped to
shreds, let the dust off
soles, a wash and gape
before you go, and then
in one fell swoop the fall
over the baresark moon.

Worse still, no starter
bust to wreck but our
platinum shade, none
the wiser, quaverings
in such heaviness for
what can't be caught
in immanence, faces
turning to some wall.

Pour on, or mould to
a ruin this stream for
fear, such cloud foes
of red, a magnet to its
dim pouts, set distant
from what slips off in
the midst as the paper
still holds out for less.

Star after star, army
of pale fleece, turn a
fiery crest in this hue
or temper as its heap
slides a berry whose
spine lies broke, one
half ripe, for lush lip
as her nom de plume.

It is so sweet, sherbet
throat, black dabs on
dorsal horns, larks of
its hired hand done to
defile even cool napes
such as yours, or rage
parked behind a desk,
but not worth its salt.

Our betters propose a
picnic, sprays of bitter
pills, what salty melon
spread over a surface
dying of brass tongue,
the mucous slab cut to
craving muscle or gone
to blaze for an instant.

A star burst, a harvest
in glass fathoms blown
to this, purple trains of
antique oral crusts, no
kidding, even sabers of
pure ideology across a
night fire, it smoulders
so and perishes in glitz.

Money slipper, a spice
so suffuses the sky of
abstract quantity that
mirth fills the evening
gall, its family breezes
loosening myelin fibre
with carping traces to
give each other the lie.

Much frayed at the edge
then, a human element
growls its militant last
ditch, their tendency to
yet finer points of open
face, saline revels, more
the merrier, rumbles or
wished still for hissing.

You take it all back, all
you ever ran through,
from frosted silver foil
to the spitting curls of
piping hot camouflage,
such fighting talk, here
where not one whiff of
rank child is left to air.

Fly me to our room of
least computed mocks,
each burden of roof to
lifts of dismal brine in
aquatinted scars, brave
drills tuning a shunned
or bouncing lunge, the
balmy night has come.

Go, then, to the rent
look where all show
of bitter ends, crust
and rosette, simmer
and knife, throws its
face to the wall, each
skipping drift of dark
in its resting clutches.

And in the red corner,
done dusted, there to
sink, as some pillow
of rested cases, each
upon its broken foam,
the plaster gives, not
in circles of the wire
but out of our hearing.

from As It Were

And out of dominion
wake the silver string
to a lowly crime rate
and bagged flat, the

first come to, nor dare
to wield, shafts from
cloudy blandishment
to some honeyed bard

made on limpid ream
array, and is no more
master of the rolls nor
of these myriad locks

Thence as to axial palms
shun the set out, a pencil
    dawn envelope, dog stall
and affiliates taken to a
steel more glitzy. Placid
is firm nearness, the licks
    of favour on of old to late
off waxen table books, the
very boudoir on slow ticks
and styles of bone in uses.

The pile driver rings
in late memo flasks,
ristretto fire, in goes
to Monday, when to

a weak shift there's
but a flower in your
open look, a feeble
task force through to

take of day, tasto solo,
this throng of down
sizes jogging holdalls
for a high water clerk

call it a day off

The larkspur gives to belly
  armour, a sheen repellent,
holding their job who reels,
more for out sourcing, o yes
  if music be, nor dance shine
sweet all, nor would go tear
to lingo, near to what will
  you do me on that, sip awry
I grant, but feel its heritage,
its cloth to warm boot loads.

22 Jennifer Moxley

Stem of the Tree of Orestes

With a nose for small
powers and their logics
I once for a long time
sat several feet up
on the misery branch
near to the wood-crack
breaking point weighted
with the old ample love
owed my mother, long
dead, and our father,
dead too as well as for-
gotten, he who willed
his worn selection
of sumptuous oblivion
to me at the onset
of my full-grown life,
and thus to the future
I then thought to begin.

At that time you said
I was heavy with
sentiment, but how
could I otherwise than
notion-made be as the
heir to an ancient debt?
Ever since that blood-
stained day when I
was gently handled,

and bid withhold
my tears, for, I was told,
he is an old man
war-torn and blind but
for his helpless fingers
feeling beneath
a cascade of clean bed-
clothes for a useless pair
of reading glasses, as if
it was of logic born that
infirmity had proved him
already cold. And she,
our mother, persisted
for her lost passion
to ask nothing—
but vengeance—for which
there will be in your heart
no forgiveness.

If in my leafy retreat
I remain, white-faced
and ever work-a-day,
mouthing retarded lies
beside my container
of unemptied dutifulness
how could you possibly
know it? And even if
each approaching Spring
you postpone your home-
coming anew and I think
to give up for good, I know
you can no more return
to find me old in an obsolete
childhood than I, once you'd
left me in this cursed house,
could have kept hope to leave.

A Transom Over Death's Door

Redemptive definitions fixed in tension my control, or then I
Wandered blind, and there's the end, the deadened idea
Of the where and the when of it, no matter the works I've read
Word for word, within the Hall of Mirrors I saw prophetic
Charioteers pulled by roosters across a bloody painted sky,
Gilded myths for future tourists, protectors of the perpetual
Court of light, some other spring this might be ink
For wreckage; but who are the poor and who are the thieves
And who are the rich and who are the thieves, and who are
The friends who will later claim the rights of primogeniture
While you are thinking, yes, from image havoc pressed upon
Your present state of mind, the whole wide world by products
Pulled apart, some hollow personage destroying my supposed
Memories of girlhood in the suburbs, and Apollo, too much beauty,
Nonluminous bodies lit by the light of the ideational particle, Am I?
What if? Is resentment but a race of repetition I do not recognize
Myself within, unlike the minor key's harmonious dirge, the instant
Contentment of the appropriate sound unfolding to an isolate ear;
Could it be? The ambient blackmail of the bourgeoisie, dialogues
Threatened, were this a real war or maneuvers in limits, a slight
Rusty patch, I'd choose misunderstanding over anti-social
Tracts in which, Truth, laurel crested beauty of the skies, attacks
Our borders once again, enemy of the stories of the story's
Undoing, bi-polar canons of experience, the long hard fight for
The right to devour, what are we going to tell the old, wasted
Mind, the irritation behind what I could possibly feel, abnegation
Atop my skull rejects the optimist's argument, common sense
Against the inner life and transubstantiation joined to shred our
Peace about us, now you see what it's like, as once I was a little girl
With no ambition but seduction until I chanced to overhear
The future, one language fitting into the next, class the common
Element, in which all futile desires quiet away in similar forms
Of loneliness and frustration, in what pursuit? Nightingales singing,
Lightless songs, Phoebus lost in the common swallow of the two
Star-crossed and helpless strangers, in a well-tempered childhood
Grave of ideas, this all took place, long before the economics of our

Interwoven failures came out into the open and I found a four-leaf
Clover, evidence enough to bring the resource question up again, well-
Fed, miserable bookishness amidst a pantheon of glorious athletes,
My hands are shivering, I miss the writing, I know what it has and has
Not given me, here where drawn-out lives grow longer in false desires
Disturbing envy and multifarious revelations of bright recycled hope.

Soleil Cou Coupé

You are born into an aptitude for original patterns,
and thus could draw figures from the balcony
of the ever translucent Milky Way should it faint
into your enormous arms, ponderous as a life once abandoned to chance.
Though bulk is another matter, such that you can barely drag
that starry chain of guidance down the street. You go out anyway,
in search of the universal key, ride a wheel in your head repeating:
"crepuscule, I could love you for resonant reasons alone."
You are worldly and dream of possibility. The dirty street
is a code of forgotten messages announcing your next performance.
People around you don't notice, they are too busy turning
the detritus of capital into flower petals, little poppies fluttering
like threadbare silk. They dance and you understand it to mean:
"Two bacchantes celebrating," as you might have poured
steady streams of rage into the name of one single betrayal.
You continue on with your composition:
"Falling plane, you are your own hellfire,
for you deny us the easy nobility of reflection,"
and so goes your tendency towards novice philosophy.
Disgusted, you promise yourself you will no longer
make a model of the pebbled pathway in the garden
though the past be a pedestal and the future in need of a map.
You will make no allowances for the misery footprint
or the anguish of love anymore, you decide you have never known thirst.

As you prepare the final touches on your ancient theory of "we,"
your ear gets caught up in the whir of the planets.
Jupiter, childhood phantasm of striated dust, demands:
"How long are you going to waste your time in idle luxury?"
Thus every stroke of brilliance becomes but a dream
and means something other than what it seems,
your reverie is just an inaccurate template forever imprinted
upon the night sky. "Let the overseers
put the remains of the earth on trial," you scream, "I'm tired of duty!"
You hurry home at dusk but fall upon a dead bird by the side of the road,
tiny pink featherless neck, sun throat slashed. From the writing desk

the workers bear witness to the destruction of your mental hideaway,
but the fight you in your imaginary thoughts provoke in them
proves nonetheless impossible to speak of. From the inkwell museum,
from the window out into the garden, from the stone fortification,
inside the grotto, cold water drips down upon your neck.
You grow weary when you realize the old world will not stay new for long
and even the dead men interrogate you, the ugliest among them
fills you with anguish and longing. They would rather look
upon the flames of your funeral pyre from out at sea than abandon
the will of their fathers. You like to suppose you will never love again.

The remains of great industry crunch under your feet
but lack the abstraction they need to be beautiful, good faith
becomes unnecessary and you leave your "desperate moment"
behind in the coffer of man's wish to be beaten. You still believe
you will find your way home. Mad, you file anger under a lack of wealth,
hurl epithets at the pale academic who attempts to make sense
of his deep, structural, loneliness by staring at the rotary
of wooden pencils held together by an elastic at the corner of his desk.
Realizing that palace, thankfully, is destroyed, you yearn for the hollow
backbone of the earth and its thrust goes straight to your head.
All around you the women give birth. They are as foreign as they are
sensuous and you, barren, cannot know their lives. You have been born
into the rhythm of conquests on an offbeat year, your art opens out
upon a vista of violence. Thinking you hear the rustle of oak leaves
you reach the end of your rope, your knife blade is pressed
to the throat of belief and trembles in fear of its conspicuous beauty.

The Easter Lesson

Some six-hundred thousand years after fire, what thinks
the noble grandson of this generation of Jules as he runs his digit
across the Bronze Age contract rusted to the face of his domicile?
Though speechless Tarvos may walk a road that leads to the Odeon
in disrepair, followed by his three crane escort, does it mean he dreams
of the apprentice poet, schooling reluctant citizens, eager for miracles,
in the art of envy? Does the poet know his only hope is a shift in
        jurisdiction,
and so await breathlessly, one bag packed, for the headwinds to gather
beneath his feet while little threads of moral gold push down
from his tired arches deep into the stones of the Panopticon?

In a shifting Empire gusts may arouse the marble folds of Livia's opulent
        dress
as she climbs the stairs of the ancient temple, yet the pantheon corpses,
frozen beneath the visitor's footsteps, are still guarded by a phalanx
of peripheral wives, bourgeois protectors of the seven arts,
who dream the "b.c." on their mantle clocks and long for the despotic
exceptionalism of their fathers. Are they possessed of the
appropriate sadness if a tear of protest falls from their eyes
for the gradually useless deities? Is their desire for unobtainable Mercury,
written in twilight entries, the same as that of the drunken soldiers
lately given sadistic leave to torture whomever they please?

There is also among them a young man wearing a Gaelic tunic
who is not necessarily a savage, though it's true he may flinch
should the spectacle proceed beautifully without dissent.
He divides his deity in threes, each segment is a form of flesh
depicting perpetual suffering. Each suffering is the best excuse
to continue on as before. Might he not yet fall asleep,
exhausted in his master's field, and dream he sees in the willow tree
his lovely wife at the cusp of dawn, above him an enormous moon,
wearing the horns of Tarvos, throws down a haunting light to reveal
the endless rows of ancient bodies layered beneath the neglected earth.

Poet, at the mid-point of our life's journey the vault will set a block to
        entry,
young in thought the world, despite these apparitions of grace, shall
        abandon you
to its discrepancies. Can you manage the small acts of sacrifice
though they bleed the matter from your life? Can you doubt what you
        are risking
when, as the lynchpin of four thousand years, you choose to provide
        the limits?

23 IAN PATTERSON

from Hardihood

1

Change sun by sun and fling and laugh
as any spot that now had fired the waste
from the bill twitted within my brain's
winter edge, shaped in slow regret.

I wrote two letters. Given words to mine
it cuts like my table carried off by name:
touchdown will carry you back unpaid
as a vane would disjoint witchery from me.

This can of shapes from the files is a spot
when he'll come equal into the streets,
as we did with a more crashing iron fire,
a little string and a working flare pane, maybe.

Flung my iron to the bushes, to the stair,
before a cupboard. Our hands, her personal
arch stood in homespun reason's blink
burst by numbers and without the walls.

Cornered or vast, what was this green grain
to the wild eye in a ferny ring,
broached to turn with self to thin sense
between yours and mine, the sun's lip upcast?

Even no sign under her pin, steel and stone
vanished and returned on the panel.
The names had failed where the mist felt the dust,
phantom hints gone for response to open.

The name changing the barren tree
to shades of irony, rapt in the true one
to her ruin from bee slumber. Mile by mile
I come to my voice, the grasp of other.

I was like a tract on every side
as I stood in a rose spot where even the new reasoning
looked radiant, breathed all our lives
in mothy walls, under archways of thought.

Now as early measure forbids writing
I conceive laughter and a light green breath
set in unrest and small ash trees. My page
is in my space, my light like silent zest.

I claim to feel I cannot find my lack
in bespoke ends, flush within that day
your body gazed and gazed far up my stair
boring within my bones, and moved things.

Drain the light wasted by sleeves in risk,
give space stairs in secret. Nettles in your bread
by the incipient lines do indeed say green
by this and skin my cold equanimity.

2

Pronounced or heard, hid here in the late spring
while red shapes of puppets circle
and rust, I'm apt to lift you back, loving as rain.

Scarce guns in their yellow kiss stood
under the arch called circumstance
yet at that time no rent was set to the years.

Rest breaks strange stars in the waning cold
of meaning, to be still as wings. Beyond earth's doings
a father broods, speaking at a spot, and on the sky.

Last and stay, cling and greet the sick men
in blue light and dim thought of zest.
Flash out a slit through chrome frippery.

Form lies in a pinch to be ecstatic
till the image raised the plot, blind and blended
with each dome to spell cove and abrade each groin.

In the day shapes sink as ripples out of nothing.
I can recall a man who died by an alley
hurled into the sun by the bloody darkness,

And crushed like a bent tune. Extinct romance
may be silent on its long trace and count as mine,
perplexed in these late tappings and distortions.

I said iron shall perish to a shining black regret
and leave some impulse missed on the eclipse
of immense human war crimes and wounds

To life, and maybe what I believe unlit with replies.
What is worse than unanswered broods in the night
Of laws which attack life, their sleep-worker and song.

3

Opened tissues feel
one wild frame from dawn
till we go to speak

Yet she never succeeds
those millions of daily messengers:

I say some scheme tore shape
by a word flash through my land

Written on the poor unconscious flesh
that I still traverse through the heat.

    4

Fear and dwindle waste the ear
No hint to fly to sense:
Ignorant skies shut earth's wide tear
And bide unreasoning yet.

Today organic dust will wane,
Be lit and unfold as this moment
Had just begun to speak
For a red cloud by the home.

When I edged a shape by this
I broke my word and left off
Biting these cheeks and bonded
With a broken time that knew it.

Between now and a guarded tongue
My face is froth, not fate:
I need to find things I knew,
A spot by no trace of old intent.

Meet me at my tread with preoccupation,
Which grew as the call for hours;
Follow my scared dead seasons
Into a thin sound screened from the eye, swallowing things.

5

In the patient world, be an instant
It subdues. Times drop their fires
And we think we drop a blind moth,
My page in space the lamp.

Know how days are birds turned to men:
Birds used to feed us shapes that cry in frost
Till delay took the shine in a mask
And the eye of strings trembled through air.

We swim on form and stony hands
As the door to less and the scarce steps:
Content is gone to name his fancy protest
Where feet mounted the will with his cameo.

Her thoughts track the sun to the lawn end
In rooms by now happier than winter:
The vent of pain is familiar, her dry ears
Wrenched to a text we half ruined.

This could have been bewitched by feathers
If thought did not cut masks with a pencil.
See that poetic water? Banks change shape best
As I look at knowledge, not you in spring.

All alight with bitter fields, the blind
Find my messenger breath gleaming red and cold
In the twigs, prone to a hurried request
To one who wrote back these eyes.

No feet bestow me where you walk beside sight,
The door emblazoned twice in the frost:
Black is best and dust has no shapes—
Matter is delight and fear, shaped in my path.

6

for Jenny

The stolen world, glowing and benighted with vision,
Ending over my ivoried task, moves and burns;
So now I draw this spot to that field in the dark
And calm all the stone time of my words.

And now the nettle did blow. It wears my fate.
I trace feet from shapes that dance
Through the night for little cost,
And shade her eyes with no repayment, no calm.

I scanned each lost child for time at his pause,
And dwindled to be left like his name:
Memory is a crumbled tree, a spectre in a mind
That may be wrong as in song the peewits grieve.

Now a rose and an arid silence heat my presence
Against the green skyline. She thought that voice spoke
Of my father, between dream and content,
Full of steep surprise, its curve wasted by sunlight.

Then the form of time did not return again?
Fifty years faced the dry tap and I heard Johnny's tale
In time to the wind as light dispersed the files,
And the plans I once had approached the tract of words.

The first voice was dead. I wondered what secret door
Went out through the fields beyond me. Can my mouth
Close while words lie within me? I sang the tune
We sang walking in the summer when form is fire.

7

for Jenny, again (Happy Birthday)

After all the breath, we were altered of heart
And at last each circumstance was mine,
The yew line to her every story consigned
To new lines and conventions within her precincts.

Spells of time may account for unregarded sea,
And then more times in the street,
In that long winter breath in the memory
Before names step in to my eyes and speech.

Dancing as we lay and moved like sparks
Of living ashes in a bower of breath,
I passed my heart and changed, smiling
More eyes with nothing beyond two.

What array of speech did they cover
Outside Paradise on the windows between!
Distance was a spot under the dark show
And will repeat your name through and through.

But O you, presence that fingers a close time
At dawn in sudden lines that die like a cloud,
The kind eyes, the thought with all it cannot blank,
Reached us sleeping, body and soul resumed.

8

You need no door with me, never the manifold tints
in some fancy life after a dead past. You are the spots
in a voice just the same as our note and the pale waves.

We burst in wild junction and slowed to something fled.
Time has been unflinching as rain says what a day thinks
just after noon in the mind and its phantom turns.

As a vision touches thought and, yes, bears eyes
that slip on jade to the door, to the dwelling where fire blows
and the sea pieces this finger, I still stand under the rooks.

You gaze from news of glass and smile about it between
my dim eyes wrapt in filmy time. Shift things from the table
and persist in words for circles and presences that see me.

Having said this, a trace of word paused before a splash
of dawn parted the horizon of things menaced by need
and its coppery march, till all was warm air and suspended here.

24 J. H. PRYNNE

from Red D Gypsum

Did you light furtive aggregate late-flow samples
to peter out frozen turns almost dive back cloven
slate, nearly slow now. Lastly lit well did you,
not yet waiting over, visibly knowing ahead blank
parts zinc plates yours. Thermal in latch fluid
image blurs selector forks, aspect sweet would my
do its wash and round lower lower still to steps
grounded for all rejoinders to miss so new a weave.

Sweeten to black taper against reverse vesper mordants
thinning to fur and fur relinquish, cap to bright oak
pause riding up and over tannic steep slants by far
fetched blazing their links. Accredit late cut dazing
underside selvage obscure, peltate divided refound as
for holding both cover traps, their links sub-ferrous
attracted to wind down: yet plumage in sport remix will
slacken by quirks of wooden converse chimeric or later.

Avail what would clamour so late. Three trammel birds
cut-out flat in fury department, have entered denied
for terror fallen off the track directly smeared,
bilobar hand signals way marking, so giving way over
to see the bones in his fingers frothing clapped up at
eye to eye birth intervals. Their three gaps gefangen
across the doorway, soaking up iron occupant sights
for a level palate, hit fresh on a low set at the back.

As for soda glass too, new tabby proof sniffing over
for tabby go down, secret mascot draggles a coat
open-cast at dark bleaches for favour to lift out
prolific partition in trio. Concede a blink beyond
supper to turn, go down, flat loading incisive sparks
left on uppermost below cover to last. All in front
out of reach to outlive frequently, why not enhancing
each new red glow in the round for water features.

Truck out black, blue shaken front by a twig blurred,
in allowance they all said, on the path. All ready
to lack nothing for a time latent, downy carbon rule
attesting, divergent on part-opened flurry pack
pressed to bank heat sunk, torn. Trailing up for
darker wads over red you said fast, green for soon
seen marking wet leafy left bruise. Yet half openly
brick by block there up, never startled by abrasion.

Unwinding zinc yellow for the reform purchase mishap
chased through in cross links snipped, parian debate
set back to winter timing. Maroon pyrite will label
the delta quilt decurrent, liking a flame in court,
a flashed partner lifted still on still. Harsh still
at a key seedling tray, every striation laps pat to it
and flickers silk latin salad flourish. The black scar
shadows overhang for lintel grips on the sash cement.

It slants back now, across the field, cladded over
its adverse retentive slipper feeding. The ruts declare
for air for stolon rising, donated in a handshake.
Its bark declining splits up a magnate loosely tied
to broach and remonstrate. Deal first arch and fair
as wheat leaves last, loping across broken furrows;
all three enter now, adding raked brow to brow and yield
in seed rated this way, arrow to hit up transfer lake.

Leaf paris green strikes a vein in the room dropped
beneath attention rode out fume trusted with layers,
run over in winded plaster cuts split from below.
Evenly screened out of line wavers no less, touch
or miss on the water black. Further notice no test
points to follow after tacitly. Blaze the way first,
on tack at base pair, the seen front sets foot down
by altered burning friable stubble already coerced.

How near the underflow locks out to a hot prism
bolus shading off massive indigo precedent come in
attaching 86 zero quip markers, over raised D flash
on its matt red square. Only counting these top-
cutting fine on edge or be may after, tripod shine
at filet gaps in your mazes, your larder. Frequent
gave them all, ready on tap radial. Three on deck
oblique partition revoked adverse germination tint.

Omission park to pack, sweet water pluck sweet wood may
dent fortune's cavity to lie low or insert the crafted
picnic trocar: too hot to grasp a spindle linking the bank.
Silent pads slide to the front, merely insinuate afresh
these alarm touches, lees in rack. Tame steaming flip
ataraxy debates on rewind panurge, hot gluten never so
picky, get resoled on redemption. Greeting announcers
touch up the fender hardly, poorly provided in benison.

25 PETER RILEY

from Excavations

119.   III

The train passing in the night, slightly shaking the structure, indi-
cates plainly that I cannot want to live. The stains on the porcelain
similarly, the spaces between the stair treads mounting to the loft,
and the row of three inner chalk mounds *in a line East-West, the only
burial being on the flat top of the central mound* head W facing S and
smiling at the very idea of living. Perhaps a traveller, a modern
politician, floating out for a term, pocket of hidden agenda *two
water-worn pebbles* and protected head. From thought perhaps. Or
the winds that bring difference, the impress of populations on the
earth. But where he finally looks, when wholeness finally covers
him in its great arc and nothing can prevent it, where wholeness
finally breaks him, and he lies in the pressed earth . . . two black
holes *to South, the further much larger* seeming to confirm, that what
he ultimately desired was to live, and didn't know where to look.
Or listen, to the passing freight, the sainfois shaking in the wind,
spots of blood on the smooth agreeable slopes.

Either/Or, the ground slants, and divides. The dictionary speaks of diremption while a soft glittering moan runs from the pavement into the national computer. Quietly, by the starred button meaning long waiting without thought of result. For people are not what we see of them, even when we see them most. ¶So a line is drawn, a straight line *a rough chalk wall from one side of the mount to the other, 50 feet long, WNW to ESE, passing some ten feet SSW of the central grave* A line separating sight from knowledge and asking no more, **love I or love I not** *the upper part of the body covered with turf, the lower part of the body covered with chalk rubble* green under white or white under green over or under Rothko's floating horizon, the earth at its fulcrum halts desire (but doesn't halt yearning)—the dictionary speaks of cadence. ¶Latin terms, sockets turned to SW and lost promises across the lawn; an elegant period, as it were by Boccherini or Wittgenstein. But to centre the entire institute by reaching a true concern across the dividing flux, full and rough as it comes: then what is lost is retained, *a bronze dagger held in the right hand, with a flint blade laid on top of it.* ¶A high voice across the fan vault and straight down to the young question on the slab, **I did but see her** and so carefully poised, asymptotic curve where the day ends and finds its object, firmly and slowly **passing by** relented gravity, moon behind hill. Circular token where lives recuperate their absence. ¶So these signature augment their worth as they traverse the entire economy hill to hill across the vale, industry and speed for what, for the core of a life that passes by. ——Messenger creature, loaded with celestine, save the earth from nugacity. Wondering what it means we hope to yet, surely.

—guaranteed hole in the forehead vast plain stretched before, of industry, or waste, sheltering nothing. The god appears at a juncture, where the possible person vanishes, leaving a space/ "... flocks of bustard and flights of dotterel and the thickets of water-loving alder" among which a thin line of thin kine and berries which is where we still live, and vanish into (the dry wine of, microtechnic pastoral.

And these streaks of phosphorus on the ground indicating paths, of exit, the dead infant giving birth to the Ancient of Days because the world can never be the same again, because a baby who did very little, next to nothing (but entirely) occasioned a naming, and a new structure, and after long perusal, a hope. Apollo's cup-bearer (clusters of knowing sinking to the heart) (an orbital route-map, the fire of delay, a dynamo) redeems all lost promises.

In my youth, at school, we were much engaged with questions of eternity. *All other burials, and there were about twenty, were at the top of the chalk mound, mostly in earth-filled (dark) hollows in the (white) surface, several with chalk flags beside, above, and over, parts of the body and head. But there were no burials in the NW segment, and the SE segment contained only children, seven of them, of which five were in a straight line to SE.* It seemed to be something out-there, a singularity, open to recognition.

Thoughts of gratified desire flew diagonally across the sky leaving the singular result untouched, lying on the ground, facing the light. As if there were an historical hope, and formal question, in the surface shine of a small prize donated to a baby. And lust formed a sign to south-east illuminating the god's vast scattered demesne, charging into dawn pursued by (a bite in the heel) generation. Meaning I fork on the outskirts of love like everyone, and go tired to bed to await the exhibited pain.

Beneath which the original transaction still holds, under all that prizing and placing under all that echo, the child-exit lies intact, at the plug-end of a "slight hollow" in the Original Ground Surface, *heavily burnt and with many animal bones strewn on it, also 79 flint saws, 17 scrapers, 3 arrowheads, 2 points* . . . this infant lies in industry (& waste, in what s/he can't use) in a hollow in society its boundless despair at the silence of boundless love—to have died, at one, out of, and into, that band of abandonment . . . . . within which a (clearing in harm at which) an agreement (every noun in the world enters and stands round the edge of the theatre, merely witness to the soul's departure to where, no-one knows, the goal of desire, the promise met, the fruited verb))) To be in position at the gates, facing the very vanishing that creates the world, like a cup to be grasped. As if the lost eyes saw

saw a crown in lowness, and a triumph in despair.

149. *Thesis.*

Where the person vanishes the god appears. There at the fulcrum of the marked space the node that empowers the tone. Bearing love like a train of falling dust and petals vanishes into a point in seeing where the power over distance resides, that commands every duty. Again and again, appears, "There, in front of you, can't you see him?" (it, genderless emanation of, an entire life at point | creates an imago at the edge of day when the light is on the turn, appears then, half visible half a contour of the closing foliage at the field's dark side. (*Eurydice, Elaine of the cold white hand!*) Appears, and never stops appearing, in the grain of the worktop, remembered honesty in speech, wherever the person's act is final and lamp . . . appears as the person departs into, because s/he must, the world. Come back we shout but it is too late, we get a certificate. Would give every god there ever was for another touch of that warm hand. *Thesis abandoned.*

169.

A small vocabulary, where North is possible or not and South is likely, and East-West runs the trade, brightening the copper wire. Then lay my profit in the ground, as a finished thing, a welcome agreed between contraries. And leave it there, departing at a particular tangent to the dialectic, turning aside from, the whole person as a line extending from a point (for we drift off the earth and everything we make is left behind us; the greatest retention an account aligned to a sector of the whole a line turning this way and that for **Musick's the cordiall of a troubl'd mind** anywhere at all. Meanwhile the sugar creeps into the berry, it's a disaster of a kind, the bass that holds the sequences, a weather front, a war, creeping down the earth.

These things are set at the edge of the balance sheet, to which no metaphor belongs; the earthline swells and closes, holding the horizon coiled like an infant in the womb, everything we were and could have been, the future never reached, is fixed at the diversion sign where war pours into the ground. Remember me.

And set my failure in the soil, that/ ebbs and flows against a **constant marke** which is | what my love remembers. My love remembers to wake me when the North sends a promise a promise down.

The word that sings out of the ground, and the sound of mourning between the shoots of (a term shifting over many centuries from "grass" to "wheat": *emmer* and the wind passing and shaking the leaves . . . *No home but the struggle* but no struggle worth half a thought that isn't to spread home across the earth, wherever the light wind creeps and the broken leaf settles, to sit there in justice. A whole and singular thing, a self. That stays a self and stays sited as the world offers faster and faster transport to nowhere in particular. And the fast transport shakes the earth until the self and the roof and the steps of the Institute slide into nonentity in a smoke, a cleansing smoke a smoke for getting rid of people. That drifts across the town most natural seeming of a Sunday afternoon, raising a smile in the ethical couple, that their dependence is full of continuing labour and the planet well mined. The smoke comes from behind a wall where some self fell an inconvenience to the great hurry.

SO (male) headless to NE "facing" SE *arms crossed in front of his diaphragm, part of someone else's skull on his knees* and what he has left to see with sees the answer, the homing pigeon settling on the loft roof, the luminary over the horizon, **Out of th'orient crystall skys** it sails! it bounds down to earth! and he knows it, his self so broken that the clearness can do no harm. In fact sacrificed, **That I may neer disdayn.** I reckon so, how about you? *A sherd covered in fingernail impressions.*

Then fall, and with an art of falling, to a state of shelter. To a history, tension of forms across the possible, written into a closed fire that arches over succession, fall exactly into that. And lie there, in more space than you need, your history forming an empty cavity offset behind your back like a rucksack as you religiously face SE and sneeze for luck. Fall no other way but back to the lapse, where nothing is surer, the core and sudden end of love. Through a thin stratum of dried blood, tomorrow turns out.

Wednesday

A beautiful morning; we go down to the arena. A
cold wintry day; we open some purse. A day is
lapsing; some of us light a cigarette. A deep mist on
the surface; the land pulls out. A dull mist comes
rolling from the west; this is our imaginary adult-
hood. A glaze has lifted; it is a delusional space. A
great dew; we spread ourselves sheet-like. A keen
wind; we're paper blown against the fence. A little
checkered at 4 PM; we dribble estrangement's sex.
A long, soaking rain; we lift the description. A ripple
ruffles the disk of a star; contact thinks. A sharp
frost and a night-fall of snow; our mind is a skin. A
slight cloud drifts contrary to the planet; the day
might be used formally to contain a record of idle-
ness. A slight storm of snow; our prosody flickers. A
solid bluish shadow consumes the day; we think
about synthetics in the night. A soul-thrilling power
hovers; we drink it back lustily. It is the exchange
of our surplus. A very great tide; lurid conditions
enter as fact. A very wet day for it; we loathe and
repeat and suckle our sentimentality. April has never
lost its leaves; our heart is both random and arbi-
trary. At sunset red and hazy; we seduce the perma-
nence. At times moderate becoming good; we'll be
voluptuously poor. Begone! facilitates our appear-
ance. We go inside rapture. It is our emotional
house: A grass green fibre of wool decking cassio-
peia. The fourth part of utopia suppressed by the

existent horizon. In the real dog hours, conspicuous splendour. The dog who all the signs name Senator. Water, wherever water comes from. Declension of the sky, the caduceus or staff. Capability of nomenclature. A crinoline covered our face. Lyres, serpents, and other luxury equipment. Conspicuous lineage of Greece. Latrines. The quorum as alibi. The sun so situated. Brilliant; equilibrium speaks mysteriously through our larynx. Checkered blue; appetite will be more likely. Cheerful, tender, civil, lilac colours; we anticipate the never-the-less. Clear blue but yellowish in the northeast; we sit and explore. Clouded towards the south; we will not be made to mean by a space. We'll do newness. Crickets accumulate; our expression of atmosphere has carnal intentions. We also do decay. Dusk invades us; the description itself must offer shelter. No gesture shuts us. Each leaf's a runnel; the struggle is not teleological. We break the jar, smack it down. Soul spills all over—cyprine. Every rill is a channel; our shelters are random. Every surface is ambitious; we excavate a non-existent era of the human. Everything is being lifted into place. Everything is illuminated; we prove inexhaustibility. Far into the night an infinite sweetness; beyond can be our model. Forget the saltiness; we tear the calendar of bitterness and sorrow. Here a streak of white, there a streak of dark; we pour the word-built world. In April as the sun enters Aries, the clouds are gold and silver dishes; we make idleness as real as possible. Isn't the hawk quite beautiful hanging quite still in the blue air? We dig deep into our conscience. It all reflects the sky; we disintegrate our facade. It anticipates the dry scent of autumn; we anticipate the same. Our emotions are slow enough to be accurate. It emits a tremulousness; we have nothing concrete. It falls in broad flakes upon the surface; we take account of all that occurs. It goes all soft and warm along the way; we are almost cozy. Is it nice having our ticket handled? Like feminine and serious sensations of being gulped. It has soaked through; we have sheer plastic virtuosity. We flood upwards into the referent. It is a protestant warmth; we reverse it. It is an illusion; we aren't afraid. It is clothed in such a mild, quiet light; we intrude on the phenomenology. It is eight o'clock; casual men shut the architecture. It is intrinsically bright; it is our middle class. Don't notice if we open the life; it is literally the wreck of jewels. It is moody, vigorous and dry; we hear the transparency. A seeing can no longer list. It is no longer the end of a season, but the beginning; the buildings make holes in the sky. What must be believed? We go backwards and forwards and there is no place. No shape is for later. It is obscurely flawed, but it really isn't. It is still daylight outside; kick out the lid. It is sun smoke; we put on grease. Our sex is a toy weather. It is the clear, magnificent, misunderstood morning; we pick up the connections. Toy weathers mean less than we assume. It is the regular dripping of twigs; we deal with technical problems. It is too strange for sorrow; we tried to make the past. It leaves behind frag-ments; we repeat the embarrassment. It screams sensation; we must be vast and blank. It seems moister; the webbing folds. It strives to pierce the fog which shuts the view; we flow through the loops. We duck into the tint. It translates Lucretius with a high rate of material loss. It turns decorative; we waste everything. It used our organs; shame was passed along. It was inevitable; we are self-regulating. It washes our beach; we resist agency. We are not free to repudiate. It will go on diffusing itself without limit; our nourishments are never habitual. It will never rain; we feel bad about certainty. It's a fine flowing haze; we don't know light. It's a tear-jerker; we practise in attics. It's almost horizontal; we seem to go into words. It's an out cropping of cumulus; we are a sum of inescapable conditions. It's been a long season; we moot the responsibility. It's brisk; we suggest a new style. It's cold in the shade; we rethink expediency. It's dark as us women; we keep up with accident. The hill slopes up. Our pearls broke. We are watching ourselves being torn. It's gorgeous; we accept the dispersal. It's just beginning; we establish an obsolescence. It's petal-caked; flow implicates us. It's so still; ease of movement is possible. It's very hot and fine; where does this success come from? It's wild; culture will fit now. It's chilly; we try to shape culminations. It's clear and windy and wakening; we achieve an inconsistency. It's starting to melt; we wander, play and sleep. Which is the surface? It's sulking behind blinds; our ideas are luxury equipment. What is beyond? Leaves shoot up; we should not remember it. Light bounces from the clouds; we play at the shelter. What's memory? Fat. Deluxe. Cheap. Listen to the pulsating leaves; everything we make is thick, fat, deluxe, cheap. Look at the moon; we reassess the lifespan of use. Look! March fans it; the conversation is flaring. We're making sounds of sincerity. Marvelous. No sun shining; we feel there must be a world. We avoid the duty of being. One hundred invented clouds multiply sincerity. You can hear radios licking nothing but the entire present, in dawdling chiaroscuro of cause and effect. You're really this classical man hearing a poem, this long voice reeling through chic traditions of green. But you flaunt privacies that split their sheaths. Like rank vegetation running you play walking like a panther when you need stimulation. It's not irony when you moisten our pen. You've always wanted poetry, our slimy harness and soft restraint. Now look; we embed ourselves in immateriality. Of course it rained! We chuck gravitas. Pinkish-green, and grey with yellow tints; look at the thin metaphor. Pockets of fog; compositions do desire. Pulsing lights; our attention is glass. Rain pelts the glass; we seek to produce delight. Skin hinges the light; this is a conceptual war. Smoke ribbons up from the city; we are splendidly desolate. Snow fills the footprints; we abruptly coincide with neurosis. Some tufts are caught in the previously bare limbs; we develop the desire. Something terrific is going to happen; we stick like belief. Space is quite subdued; but not as a result of complacency. It is the great middlediction of concupiscence. Speakable; utility. Spectacular; desolation. Spring seems begun; we like bad palliatives. Storms do occur; manifestoes are the opposite. That's right; disgust is fatal. Enough of the least. Death is a content. The air seems flushed with tenderness; prognostics give us logic. The atmosphere recedes; we simulate failures. The bay's pretty choppy; we allow ourselves to be drawn in. The blue cleansed or swabbed; we are not mimetic. We rhyme. The coldness is purifying; we create an immanent disaster. We shorten the dark. The dark drinks the light; we omitted the beginning. The day is longer now; we're fueled by the thoughtless. The dry light has never shone on it; we excerpt effort. The earth goes gyrating ahead; we frighten the strengths. The fading woods seem mourning in the autumn wind; we don't regret error. It is our emotional house. The fog is settling in; we're sardonic. The fresher breeze rustles the oak; our treachery is beautiful. Pop groups say love phonemes. We suddenly transform to the person. The hills fling down shadow; we fling down shadow. The horizon is awkward; we fling down shadow. The horizon melts away; this was the dictation. The ice cracks with a din; very frustrating. The leaves are beginning; it unifies nothing. The light lies intact and folded; we open and shout. The light seems whimsical; it's techno-intellectual work. The light's so romantic; we permit the survival of syntax. The little aconite peeps its yellow flowers; we manipulate texture. The moon is faintly gleaming; we expose our insufficiency. Total insignificance of lyric. That's what we adore. The mountains have vanished; our mind becomes sharp. The mountains unfurl long shadow; ornament is no crime. The nightreading girls are thinking by their lamps; we make use of their work. We cannot contain our pleasure. The rain has loosened; we engage our imagination. The sentence opens inexpensively; we imagine its silence. The shrubs and fences begin to darken; we are deformed by everything. Therefore we're mystic. The sky is closing in; we mediate an affect. The sky is curved downward; we desituate memory. The sky is dominant; we lop off the image. We come upon our thought. The sky is lusty; so are we. We prove inexhaustibility. The sky is mauve lucite; we reduce it to logic. The sky is packed; it is ours. The sky is thickening; we have been invented. We are the desuetude of function. The sky's tolerably liberal; despite and because of the rhetoric. The snowdrops are starting; we risk causing suffering. The snow going off; by way of the idea. The songsparrow heard; our artifice collides. The sound settles like jargon; we do not agree. The storm is a mass of sound; we must go to the suburbs. The sun is just appearing; we cannot sit waiting. The sun sucks up the steam; it is explicitly our preference. The system shines with uninterrupted light; we generate limpid fact. The systems revolve at an even pace; fear is not harmful. The time is always still eventide; our language moves across. The trees are stripped; foreground fiercely smashing the mouth. The trees look like airy creatures; we'll say any thing like speech. The wind has lulled; we're this long voice under fluid. The wind has stripped some nearly bare; we demonstrate abstinence. The wind hasn't shifted; we have shifted. The word *double* is written on our forehead. The wind opens the trees; art is too slow. The wind shifts from northeast and east to northwest and south; we cull the obedience. The wind sounds like paper; our sex is no problem. The elms are as green and as fresh as the oaks; we taste of aerial fluids and drugs. There are curious crystallizations; we are the dream of conflict. There goes the sun; we influence contingency. There is something in the refined and elastic air; we step into the quorum. They are quietly dissolved in the haze; we quietly erect this subject. Thin, fleshy roots of light; we thicken to slang. This greyness is constant; we withdraw unexceptionally. This is a cloudburst; no-one's turn is dwelling. This somber drizzle is familiar; it's unbuilding pixels. This transparency is necessary; there is no transgression possible. Those stupendous masses of cloud! We furrow and sleek and fondle our sentimentality. Thunder in the north; we enjoy our behaviours. Thunder, far to the south; habitual. Today has everything; we are sick with sincerity. Transparent tissues hover; authority flows into us. Try to remember the heavy August heat; we cannot disengage our calculations. Under that rod of sky is our breath; we don't understand love. Describe it again. Up goes the smoke quietly as the dew exhales; it calls itself sadness. Pattern undercuts the slamming heat; we speak into the dark and make corrections: Shadow for Hour. Tantrum for Lyre. Lure for Light. Rapture for Kaput. For for Five. Qualm for Finger. Bridge for Door. Neap for Note. Curious for Lucid. Door for Bridge. Feather for Epsom. Minus for Nimble. Parity for Rapture. Plumb for Addle. Rustic for Cunt. Note for Iota. Item for Opus. Rustle for Campus. Augustine for Aconite. Similar for Ribald. Firm for Forsythia. Resplendent for Respond. Cause for Quote. Oblique for Oblique. Verb for Flex. Superb obedience really exists. When accuracy comes it is not annihilated; we're economical with our sensation. Who has not admired the twelve hours? We offer prognostics. Red sky at night, a warm arm across the pillow, within winter, but at its end; you can anticipate the wind.

Brief To Butterick

The tooth of time is black to the root . . .
I have done all I could
to appear mirthful

About suffering we are always wrong.
It doesn't dawn on us what day it is —
who shave our children's heads like frigate birds
subversively, as scholarships to Dreadnaught Street,
as waxwings, as envelopes . . .
                                        and Allusion
is use
            but that which is not
                                    stills something.

Why should a dog a rat?
who cannot write. Why should a poet laureate
nationalized and public
                                have TV breath
old boy piss
                    retiring to his Connecticut
pasture, some alumnus to be
the rector of poetry
                            to play some tennis
while he can and putter around
his garden, waiting for a poem
to hit him on the head.

Looking for them we are a zoo.
Our faces halve our heads, the song
sticks and it collapses—
                    No poem
will hit no one no head no more.

Which is the letter of the letters' letter,
now reduced and deferred. Why should Bankier
Bartlett, Benson, Bergé, Berkson, Bernstein, Bertholf
Boone, Brainard, Bromige, Bukowski, Burke have use
of letters, which will be outculled

And the grass breathe on something instantly amiss
like a molecule for a season
or a monarch butterfly in love with vessels

Still, in the midst of the mess
there are intervals of life
and the heavenly bodies that dissolve at night
they are not casual in their demand for Strega
for they have come to cook up something more
than a cauldron of feathers—
loathsome particulars of afterwards.

The writer says he hopes that Ingram reads this
rather than that high-hatted rabbit at his tea party.
For pep flickers in the step down to Sukey's
at the pond's edge, where *Martz* lives (Louis?
George wonders) among the freezing molecules.

Then who could gather all those sources,
who could read all that Carl Sauer and turn
the max into an ark, no bigger
an exemplary and its repartee.

The line packed and shipped now to us all.
While the grasshopper invasion
reaches Biblical proportions
and our headless body may be that
of the lost witness
                              subject to deterioration
from the weather
                              and mutilation from animals
and other editors of the body
                    As the obituary
arrives with the new Norton
                              replacing
Oppen and Riding with pinafores

—insult were it not negligible to the trade—

While friends and poets carry on
their tedious wars at the backs
of magazines and institutions
and language associations go wall-eyed
with a view to canons and the chair
is being dubbed by a colleague
                              the rest
of the world continues its bout
with death and sloppiness
which is the rest of the world.

As though the whole thing hangs on the color of a vowel

You made the car that goes from there to here
you sharpened with pencil and an eye

the animal devouring teeth that speak
and we who still can say, know what increase
what cease, prowling among the accidents.

For there is tempest, screendoor, passport, sea:
plainest model, earth's dusty guest who gossiped not.
Young winner, function—shaper—catholic
strider who built the deck, expounded history
and its letter of projected bric-a-brac

a ship that scholars float on now
with us, out to sea in the city street . . .

    7/29/88
    Berkeley

Stewed and Fraught with Birds
for PA

Oafs emit the fundament
                on beaver board
       flung to capsules
mistaken for supposition

The French like their medicine
                up the wazoo
       as it gets to the livers
quicker than a speeding bullet

Of course DELEUZE
                leapt toward his lost breath
       counterfeit and discrete in
his choice of suicide by ventilation

Towards the courtyard like any other
                thoughtful smoker, not the street
       more vague than tall buildings and taught
to be a vertical philosopher at last

Socket, sill, lunge and shutter
                wrench the lobes
       scrutinized for links
of two—of clock face in his case

Times change and lo, time changes
                though a glass of wine
       looks the same, like Paris
where babies still are made to mold

We understand the bus of alcohol
                is dangerous
       a tobacco for saintliness
though consummate à la mode always

Some reason to write in order to read
              smoking a Chesterfield
       for Queer theory
appointed to the emphysemantic company at hand

Pregnancy's the only job worth having
              when to be set free
       is the proverbial function of the truth
which leads quicker to death than nature

Descartes had it right
              with his socks
       before those fires in the country
and the desire to think in writing

When some bar has heat we sit
              vertical instrument whiskey
       which perched reasonably
we stay awhile

You have a better idea
              write
       it down.
If not down get richly dark

The ligaments
              of your phraseology
       will eventually get
put to some truth test or other

and you'll be lucky
              if anyone reads
       it with a big guffaw
or sneezes

My future daughter or son
                    could undergo
          a bone marrow transplant before birth
even if he she has my profile or not

I guess we know
                    how wonderful
          life can be
at the end of the 20th century

not far from l'Étoile
                    Invalides or the Champ de Mars
          in a rent-controlled apartment without
a Dubuffet in the quinzième

Was it then you got up
                    on the wrong
          side of the bed?
"Yes, I did. My side."

When some foam MAY
                    be agogger
          than other foam, go for it
depending on which side of the bed sits

well with you
                    rabbit warren
          in an armchair
at the postmodern Detroit of choice

or FORCE:
                    what power suits
          it, what chance
can still illuminate the happenstance

short of course of the de rigueur
            sleeveless black leather
      vest of academe
that reveals its brainy muscles at the conference

Ahem, when I hear the words
            oh poesie
      I reach for my pyjamas
and punch out the pillows in the living room

Comedy in France
            is an honored
      tradition now
bereft of laughter

Caca boudin clinks
            the intestinal skin
      of its institution
then slides down the gullet on its own sleeve

to be noted later, still enamelled
            at the back of sulfurous magazines
      by some Beelzebub
looking for a contract on the Faust of the moment

For tons of recent trade
            will cover o'er
      this fatuous skirmish
in the next literary war

Bonne Année anyway
            to all troglodytes
      now that anti-semitism
can be a racist analysis

and post-modernism net
            and yahoo may become
        social realism at last
as modernism was reactionary by definition

Readers will see
            what I am
        driving at
though I may not have a valid license

Our pockets need some rocks
            will sink us sound
        into the three-meter width
of the Ouse

Already there's not enough
            and not enough is more
        than enough and too much
is just enough already

I wouldn't mind a future on
            another virago
        or a Harley Sportster
to fly out upon

That's my plan
            anyway, peuple roi,
        and you can sit still
on the buddy seat—I've got the extra helmet

If you put your arms
            'round my waist
        I will be
helpful to you when we arrive

Peel through the hot air belted
              with the latest naked emperors.
        Give the boys a sweater to match the girls
and undress the pretenders, to reveal the Dauphin

Even should we crash
              at the plastic bourne
        and our rugsters still
prepare at school for their career

something will be ready and in store
              at the princely corner.
        Is free falling truth the next beauty queen?
Whatever sets you free can snore for both of us

although our dumb, unidentified birds
              I see are still
        fraught and stewed
with feathers of indentified *liberté*

28 GIG RYAN

Pure and Applied

1.

The channel caves in his hand like a weak cushion
as news reads the screen
and curved along its poverty, a reflecting and equivalent desert
occupies geometry
which devalues each tincture my chatelaine
which people vacancy
like today's harping and the litmus of his hair

2.

Politicians nod like priests
You slip in the crowded chair like 3 million others
TV shows you
The rest is dreck, a slump
You surrender to his embalming pill
his glorious forgotten blockout kiss and nest
The walls' diagrams arrowing to a former heaven peter in the
        mind
Monotonous branches scratch the ditchy air
I had to look at 800 dollars
but death precedes me entering like worthlessness

3. (the good weekend)

Ten pages on a headache A world satisfied by charisma
The corner shop's dim globes the newspaper's parting atoms
but death can be "egotistical, manipulative", his claim and
      corona
Her burying mother acridly grinds into the present
An article probes the shops, the ultras
in the sad dark regions and recesses of his relation

The sheets wind milky green
and then a big blue sky's supposed to incize
putting you in the right counsel
I watch his weakness strive and shut
as theory wades, but on practice it's a klutz
I protect him from ardour
Here, in this propensity, this rust
My paraphernalia crash in a junction of boredom

4.

Automatically he'd be a lump
The light's suicide split craving beneath the wax door
Piano tinkles over the woolknit-lounge ad, his thoughts
that mirror a wreath of gloss abrupt pages
perspex and disheartened and foam
dead desire
and he uncrumples from the black lacquer

5. (sum)

"It bores me severely
Everything you say is thrashed into a refrained verdict
numbfully secure at its post
The car's underwater the doorkey starts
and recedes like a gun, excellently
and never loved. Obstruct, by all means, any silent rack or behest

Anyway, it was major which you blasted, a real user
He was glamourized, delta'd, totally miami'd
like a shoot-out, you know, head above water
His blue hair shining like rockets
Dance-a-rama *I'll* say, you should've seen the gronks
they turned away in squadrons, rapturously
to the new spasmic floor. I could've killed
but I dropped stuff instead
and was, subsequently, messed for any social, being severely
      zomboid
Last night: what a crack"

Achilleus to Odysseus

Vanished day,
to strive for fame, to glitter in a marble pool
but lose the task
You sit among the virtuous weeding out life
Personalities sulk
the talking breakfast, the blacked-out calendar
They whirl and fit

I wish I lived with silence
black waves plucking the shore away from things
Traffic stripes night and trains kick
the black dissolving world
and stove-white pages
Drunken introverts graft home
the active and idle
Velvet bodies forming on the beach
Footsteps break the slab of flats
I walk into a house of death

The Global Rewards Redemption Centre

I heal the ramparts of the deponent tense
I am being loved and certain
A toast to the surgeon's art who cut me
from her skin
The night's software: a drink

I continue my existence as a negative role-model
bathing in the blood of others
sitting in a cone of noise

Birds sing me to sleep at dawn
when you walk in the fabulous cold.

2.

across remnants of life
The spiritualist junkies examine their dreams
Nice days pass my window like a train
You follow him into the baptistery or chancellery
a guide for each muted circle
The city's crumbling brocade and souvenir
immortal art
Aluminium pillars shimmer in the bank's foyer
Sail towards the coast
Await the unpassable sorrow

Epilogue

1.

His money-making properties come back like a beach
the saintly applications
promoting Australia
Stretched logos bracelet and peck
The Assembly of Experts sits
under exit-coloured roofbeams
adumbrated, the brocade trees,
inappropriate, unloved

2.

She married her and betrayed him
Faithful knight
Hitched in the car's stifling air
I mope in my truck
World leaders coagulate support
Plough through sugared windows, shops
lilac roses, blue trees
after shining in the shadow of the last government
the heart's melted disk would have forgotten
tanked in the jumbled city
It's summer after the rain
I read the historical novels and the hedge funds wilt

3.

Coated in plastic
the newsreader head prefects' amusing formula
that writes himself off
Extinct species fidget in the wired yard
Later you remember
chained to my clock
Unable to continue I prefer really
Sunset's golden wedge slows the horizon like a door

4.

and wear the arrows of your criticism
and empty cup
and wander through the cute waterfall
Enamelled birch tree and broken canvas
Teach me to write
Buildings drift into sky over the reeled sea
and carry the load of separation
and sunset's hinge

La Penserosa

Melancholic dandy, you weep and cut
with yearning
Uninterrupted argument, truncated simile
swathed in religion's cold abstract love
The roped bridge's bracelet of light
but shadows cross your face
Paintings slide off into her text, unsolaced
in the porous flat
The past is wagging at your sloth
Responsibilities stagger in a pile
garbled head and licking nightmares
weeping at your wrist
The works don't hang anymore
They wallow in their primitive fables,
diligent acolytes
Who pulls me into the world

You'd prefer to not talk
in the ruffled hours
and shut down, away from their distracting company
The private prison opens its cells for business
The corporation welcomes the inquiry
Inside I was panicking
conglomerate regret
and putrid day levitating
Before the rain, birds whistle
as you become a statue
they mate and peck on.

29 JOHN TRANTER

from Blackout

∾

Thunder heard—speak to ourselves,
play the men. Hear him?
Assist the counsellor; use your authority;
make yourself ready
                I say.
Miserable howling!
I felt justified in experimenting.
We are less afraid
as leaky
             her two wet mouths
Paradise-blue baboon lusts
merely cheated
my wife.

∾

Wild stinking fire, love and death
in the golden land. Brave cry;
master of meddle pluck my eyes;
hair inquisition, concluding 'Stay.'
Obey five women in the dark power—
a little mirror.
No worse, foul girl; manage my liberal arts,
a stencilled white number;
study the government secret studies,

how to trash new creatures, officer.
They're not prisoners. What tune
hid my trunk? My mind
all popular, my false revenue,
my memory, indeed, would cure deafness.

To have no needs . . .
                              dry annual stooping.

Mark his brother.
He has just hooked down five dexedrines.

My grandmother—good enemy—
was treacherous one midnight—
darkness hurried me—eyes destroy my tale—
the phoney telephone men, the cops—

my people bore me; bloody business!
Foul carcass rats have quit it,
bouncing and grinding along
through the brown dust, loving wrong.

Preserve me! Smile, stomach,
beating your reason upon a star,
a confetti of skulls and desert;
cease questions; dullness, and choose
an attack of paranoia.

Fly, swim, dive into the fire,
strong quality to every article—the drive-ins,
mobile home parks, septic tank developments,
raw concrete service station toilets, plaid car coats . . .

I deck, in amazement, and burn and flame
distinctly, then tremble, my mad son,
with hair like reeds, the devils close by—
waitresses looking like milky cellophane,
their garments cooling in this sad nook, where once

midnight hid; all asleep; and the trumpets
always dropping off the note.
Is there more moody liberty?

                                     No more!
Remember I told lies, malignant age
hearing commands, refusing rage.
Then breasts undo art entrails.
Say what—

                        what shall I do?
Eyeball diligence! They will pay dearly
for the bullshit ambiance. Shake fire, profit business—
poisonous devil, wicked cramps, night work, eat berries
that burn by day and night, secret poisonous orchid;
and then sipping beer and smoking many joints,
filth violate gabble like brutish words that learn
this rock, a prison, the red language!

Roar, tremble, pray,

                        obey.

His art invisible, following yellow sands,
have kissed, bear dogs strutting,
my music gone. No, again lies;
his strange sound above me. The eye
looks about! It carries the grief, that's divine;
for I saw the daughter wrong a man, a virgin,
so great, a kind of brooding beauty,
and a spy—she wants to do this thing, but she does it
without belief. I am a man. He's a traitor. Follow.

No; I will resist such power.

                        He's fearful.

Hush! No more shapes, moving the dark angels,
the subtropical twilights and soft westerlies
off the Pacific—nerves again, so much fire
concealed by the dark. My weakness,

threats in prison. A lot of people
had been worried that he was dead.
Every voice seems a scream.

                              Come on.

∼

Hang up a yellow shirt—you cause joy;
our escape is common; every day, some wife
masters our theme of preservation,
millions speak like us.

The visitor, he will strike the entertainer.
A dollar comes to him, you have taken his tongue,
the old laughter, though
that tawny eye of green misses
the truth totally, it was crazy, a kind of power.

She was the miraculous impossible matter.
We were as fresh as your daughter,
who is my sort. Your daughter's ears
against the stomach—her strange fish.

Thank yourself, bless your daughter, lose
an African—where is your eye?
Cause the grief to bow. Fear for ever,
prickly dread wherever the wind blows.
We bring men to your own loss.

You lack some time to speak, you rub the plaster.
Very well. And when you are very foul,
being drunk, no traffic, poverty of contract,
bound metal, or oil;
no men and women, no sweat.

Knife, gun, engine: prosper in the dry air,
feed my people. No subjects govern the age.

It is possible to live and die
without ever meeting a Catholic or a Jew.
Do you talk to these gentlemen?
They always laugh at nothing.
No one remembers the past—then go. I am heavy.
He talked about metaphysical paranoia—Shut up!

What a strange climate; glossy greenery
of nightmare, then my spirits fell by thunder.
What might I see in my head?
A place for snakes to breed. Do you hear me?

                                    I do; and it is language,
and sleep.
                    What is it?
                                    This is strange, eyes open;
yet more serious than standing water.
Ebbing men near the bottom,
by their own birth, yield.

Although this memory is persuaded he's a spirit,
as he sleeps, I have another way: a hope, a wink,
he's gone.

Then tell me, who's beyond the sun?
Cry out—wake—he that sleeps
can amply make a deep chat.
O, you bore! What advancement!
Do you understand?
                            I do.
While you wink, the cat laps milk; we say the hour.

Dear precedent; I'll come free from love.
They talk, invisible; music and danger send me forth
to keep them snoring—keep care, beware
confidence of strange pygmy angel tribes.

The moon was dark and the wind was blowing.

We heard a hollow burst like bulls. It struck
a monster's ear, to make a humming, a strange one,
which cried; as I saw their weapons
there was a noise—that's our guard,
sobbing and incoherent. Quit our weapons,
for my poor beasts shall know what I have done.

~

A burden of noise, of infections
sucks up a disease! The temper of fury
has broken out among us. Hear me, and curse.
But pinch me in the dark, unless apes
chatter at me, and after their pricks hiss.
Here comes a spirit—he smells ancient and strange.
In England a holiday fool would give this monster
a dead Indian. Again, my best way
is to creep about. A man with strange dregs
singing; a bottle in his hand:

No more death, no more heartaches!
I shall die to sing at a funeral; my comfort!
Then here's my comfort—

what's the matter, savages?
Do not torment me, I'll bring his fit
now, after the bottle; drunk, it will fit.
If I can recover, and take too much.

Little wilt, trembling; open your mouth—
here is that cat. Open your mouth; this will
tell who's your friend. Open your chaps again.

I know that voice; these are devils—
two voices—a delicate voice, to speak well,
his friend backward to foul wine.
My bottle will help. This is a devil—touch me,

and eye these little devils: the siege of this moon
killed with thunder—I hid under the dead moon
for fear of the living. Do not turn my stomach,
brave god, and I'll swear to be true.
Here—swear like a duck.
                               Kiss the book.
A duck like a rock, wine from heaven I assure the man,
when time was in her, and showed me dog and bush.
Swear to the book.
                        I will swear.
This light is a very shallow—be my god.
When God's asleep he'll kiss; come on down,
and laugh. Death in my heart, in drink that I serve!
Lead the way, again.

     ∼

Some sports are odious, but
I serve what's dead, and my pleasure's gentle.
Her father, he's composed of thousands of these logs,
and weeps when these thoughts enter at a distance,
unseen. Now, work the lightning,
set it down and rest—now he's safe.
Give me that—no, you sit. Poor worm—
you look fresh at night. What is your name?

I have admired the world!
Some defect put it to the creature.
I do not know my sex; and my features are my jewel.
I would not form a shape too wildly, and I
forget my condition, this wooden slavery, my mouth.
Speak: make me patient.
                          Do you love me?
Witness this sound, I speak hollowly!
I am a fool.

I am glad. I take what I want.
But this seeks to hide itself, the cunning innocence!

∾

Tell me we will drink water, and drink to me.
The folly of this state—eyes should be brave.
In case a constable was there, tell a lie—
but how he let him, such a natural!
Bite a tongue, prove a tree!
My subject shall be the suit I made.

Kneel and repeat it;
I will stand invisible—I am a tyrant.

The monkey would destroy your teeth.
I said nothing.
              Mum, then,
and no more from me.

Trapped Wind

To Alfred Tennyson, Lester Young and Jack Spicer

Lament the harp that in its casement broods
Dumb for lack of wind, for being human
Signs escape you. But when the breeze intrudes,

Its sighing tells an all-too-human tale; boy
Meets girl, signifier meets signified,
Boy falls in love with signifier . . . Toy

Or tarry as you must, but clouds will burst;
For being human, signs escape you crying
Of course that there is no escape. Who durst

Come tapping at the casement? *Help me! I
Am Moth-Man! Hel-* Too late. The world is cold
The swifter to heal over, carelessly

Careful of its carful of key players.
Top dog in the food-chain Night's barking again
Though the same moon agitates all our prayers

For safety, who share most in truth the things
Known least about ourselves, the dark side of
The same interior stars. A wristwatch pings.

An owl. Some late cars cough. *Easy Does It*,
A coffin full of glitter spilled in space.
Then all's downloaded. Press Esc to exit,

Toll the bell and wind the harp. Aim to sleep tight,
But children's children's children's children don't—
So, up again at 3 am to write

An infant crying for the light
An infant crying in the night
And with no language but that night

What's Wrong

What's wrong with this <u>What's Wrong with this Picture</u> picture,
To lean momentarily for support on marks that pit the surface
Of the flood, as an antediluvian argument about depth
Being an illusion like negativity gets more and more deeply caught
Up in the toils and feints of its own progress, while progress itself
Surfaces awkwardly in the guise of a concept that has died, like a
    mermaid
Saying hello to a new politics, rescued from the weeds that clogged
The old, the rusted self-absorption with its quite fantastic patina,
Abruptly to surge, like that feeling in dreams of a power-surge
That is frequently the first sign of impending wakefulness, and
Then the dreamer rises, head breaking the surface of sleep to find only
Breakdown, tears streaming like currency endlessly away,
Is what's wrong with this <u>What's Wrong with this Society</u> society,
Which meets so irregularly as hardly to matter, pitting all the old
Arguments about the reconfiguration of labour as more than toil,
When abruptly the picture of an unalienated model of work, no longer
Antediluvian and certainly more real than the grail of the old fantastic
    politics
Rescued like some sort of mermaid or rusted trove only in dreams
About power in the guise of the concept of progress,
Troubles, breaking through all the surface illusions and feints
To flood, and again the tears begin to stream, and what seemed to have
Died is now rescued without any clogged self-absorption, without
    negativity,
And—combing the wreck of society for support, or just currency—jabs
The first awkward feints, breathes the first sign of an impending
    wakefulness.

Distance Learning

He seemed to have been walking forever
Up the green lane, along the narrow lane
He seemed to have been walking forever

Along the green lane where it twisted and looped
He came at last to a pane of glass
The size of a mousehole in a house that sighed
And quivered, as he stooped

To look inside. And there, in a bare sunlit
Room hardly larger than your hand
Stood, gravely, a rook
Who raised reluctantly one stygian velvet wing

And there between the feathers gleamed
The gold band of a ring.
Inside the ring there ran an endless corridor
Of blue, and at its end, a zigzag flue.

He climbed in, fell through space then found
Himself at last on a revolving stage
Bare, except for where a spotlight fell
On a single rose. He sped through the heart

Until he reached its smouldering, cold core
And there amid the breath of rustling ashes found
A door, then another, when suddenly
He thought he could smell the sea

And there fell from the air a silver shell
With a folded scroll inside,
Which he unrolled, and on which he found written
In a graceful and oddly familiar hand,

Protect your clothes from exploiting you.

Horace Belisha

Horace Belisha was briefly Minister of Transport in the wartime Government of National Caligari. Following the cessation of hostilities in 1945 he returned to the Cabinet after the then PM, Ben Sinister, pressed the wrong button at the official opening of Windscale nuclear power station and turned it into a raging Sellafield. The lights went out all over Britain, and matches — renamed 'lucifers' — were the only means at the discretion of ordinary working people to find their way about. Horace had a burning conviction of the need for sociable justice, if necessary through the supervised redistribution of wealth around the hearth. This burning had its roots in a childhood episode. He had seen minors (as the children of miners were called) queuing for bread in a depression only to be mowed down by troops on horseback unleashed at the discretion of Ben Sinister. As himself the child of relatively effluent peers he felt a knocking guilt and urge. The realisation of his ambitions came in the form of the 'Belisha Beacon', a globe of light at the end of each crossing warning minors and motorists alike of an impending cross. How much more satisfying to be remembered for creating something tangible and life saving like that than for mean memoranda and flimflam. And yet, sat in his office late at night, overlooking the manifold lucifers and lights of the metropolis — so many of them his own beacons — he still felt a creeping sense of darkness. Ben Sinister was long gone, the tall clock of Parliament that boomed so authentically and that bore his name, his only legacy. (Sinister had resigned, worn down by Suzy's crises and her interminable affairs with Lord Booby, a foam associate of The Craze.) But Horace still felt somehow implicated in an undissolved mystery of gilt and harsh munitions. He had never raised a hand against the minors, or hoarded an extreme, but still he felt somehow ostensible.

2

One day when the burtons of office weighed with a particular heaviness, Horace paid a visit to 'Blind' Butler, the legendary head of the civil service, and the real-life source for the characters M, Oddjob, Goldfinger and Miss Moneypenny in the Bond films. Blind Butler was the nattiest political poker-player of his generation, and always kept his cards close to his chest, which added provocation by forcing him to play the cards 'blind', while warming his manifold boobies. When Horace knocked at the door high above Pall Mall (where particular people congregate) it swung open and then closed behind him, seemingly at its own discretion. He advanced slowly in the stygian gloom to a desk at a window by whose noncommittal light he thought he deserved a humped and sphynx-like figure. After sitting down awkwardly and clearing his throat, Horace asked thirty-three questions of ascending difficulty and each time, after a ten-minute pause, received the answer, "*Red Box*". The two sat for a further silent hour, while darkness deepened. Eventually Horace rose, placed a working model of his beacon on Butler's desk, and left the room.

3

After a lapse of many years, I saw Horace Belisha on one further occasion. The IRA were in town making a documentary and so it was a red nose day. Mounted pleas had cordoned off Jekyll and Hyde Park, while robot hands went groping for the booby prize. Around the Park the cars raced bumper to bumper. Horace looked at the Porsches, Emphysemas and the new Sinisters with their warrior drivers and threadneedle upholstery. Then he caught sight of a ragged band of minors, forced off the road and walking by the railings under a gagging order from the fumes, who would never own such a car but might well be knocked back by one. The Belisha Beacons had long ago been phased out. Horace cut out a profile shot of himself from his obituary in the morning paper, and slipped it under the windscale wipers of a parked BMW. Then he curled into a ball on the pavement, as tight as he could, and wished himself away. Away. *Away*

from English Music

7

This was the real England, that still lives on, a fading tapestry so beautiful no-one can bear to look at it for long, for fear of tears rising, for fear that a too-sharp exhalation or simply the gaze itself might risk tearing that fabric beyond price; an England of long shadows, cricket, warm beer, and elderly spinsters cycling through the mists to evensong only to be caught and smashed beneath the wheels of a perfectly adorable little container lorry fresh from the Hook of Holland. Safeways fruit tasting faintly of cardboard wobbles lightly as the brakes scream. In my day we were taught that good manners cost nothing, that a gentleman always rises when entering a lady and that never, *never* should one so abandon all responsibility and decorum as to spill one's guts across the central reservation. Anna giggles, blowing huge smoke rings over the Home Counties. As a motorway cop in RayBans and leatherman gear approaches the corpse it rises oozing guttural maledictions and leering somewhat grabs him by the testes. I was sure the Tennyson Centre was around here somewhere. A white-haired shadow roaming like a dream. His walkie-talkie hits the tarmac and explodes into a thousand larvae, half in tiny double-breasted suits, half singing Candle in the Wind in a charitython vibrato and prancing like Tiller Girls. A naval helicopter strafes the scene, scavenging for mondegreens. I board the ghost train, and I pay the rent. Alone and silently, Princess Margaret raises her blazing white glass in diagonal shadows.

Anna wanted to show you some more of her, more of our, special things. The chimney clocks and the inlaid knuckle box; the dog that talks and the Queen's Beast that walks. The trouble was, I suppose, that they were never really ours, not to own. Even the silence is

> torn off in measurable strips
>> with a faintly audible click of impatience

while the scene changes to a teaching hospital. In the labour ward, mothers and midwives are doing fine. Then a young male doctor or even worse an old one enters and takes charge. *What an amazing world! People popping out of each other!* He stares wildly round the room, shoulders heaving with silent laughter. He marches down the ward, inadvertently yanking out an epidural then pulling the plug on twins born prematurely. Their moth-breath fades away without complaint. He stares down at a whimpering mother giving birth. *And what do you think you're doing?* To a nurse: *Give that woman potassium permanganate!* Shaking with laughter he leans too far backwards and falls out of the window. It is immediately autumn, sepia tints lanced by diagonal white light. Out on the artificial lake the doctor sits hunched in a rowing boat, whispering to his twin, a mouldering corpse with pager flashing on his blazer. But that was in the early years, before he became so difficult to work with. Lou was always into mindgames. Everyone was either running scared on the spot or cuddled up to truth in dreams as if they were bestest friends, you and I lost in the land of stillborn clouds and phantom clocks with spinning fingers, never born enough to know, but still you know the rest.

9

Sometimes the dials on Anna's magnificent machinery would be set incorrectly, and with only the briefest metallic whirr of warning we would find ourselves caught in the most undesirable historical narratives.

Once I found myself trapped in a sort of CP Snow novel. Some of the Fellows of my old College had clubbed together to build an atomic bomb, and wrote to me care of my London club to see if I wanted 'in'. Lately my life had seemed stuck in what you might call a rut, and this promised to be just the sort of caper to get the old juices flowing, with the briefest metallic whirr. Slightly to my surprise my wife needed no persuading, and we were soon standing expectantly on the platform at King's Cross wreathed in steam from the late 1950s while little men in peaked caps blew whistles, and pigeons flapped up through rusting girders into soot and sunlight.

I was not surprised to find that plans among the group were pretty far advanced. We would meet by night, standing in a ring in the carpark that is now Trinity Great Court while our hair came away in the sharp Fenland wind and our pipes stood out, fully two-dimensional. So intimate were our exchanges that the need for speech faded, as did the need for facial movement, a process (like so many) initiated at public school. We restricted our intercourse to certain mumbled signifiers of studied neutrality, alternating with shrill ejaculations of disdain. Between us we had need of only one eye, which we passed around. One particularly cold December night the Head Porter appeared in the centre of our circle and, as an act of charity, gently pulled each man's lower lip up and over the back of his head so as to form what he termed (rather unctuously, I thought) a warming pink hood. We petitioned the Master to have him put down. Successfully, as it turned out.

Our home lives were another and perhaps less interesting story. Rigsby, the real boffin in our little group, had inserted in each of our brains a zinc lozenge about the size of a cigarette card. Every Friday night, suitably fuelled by g and t, each man would bear down on his spouse—coifed that day at Madame A's, a hair salon owned jointly by Magdalene College and the Chinese Triads—for connubial duty, while the lozenge set off mental instamatics of the prettier Repton boys (or amputee pensioners, in my case). Only once did evidence surface of a 'private' life behind or instead of our agreed 'home' life. Once again it was Rigsby who haled me as I was standing up to my neck in the Cam with two retired lollipop ladies, conducting a spot of private research. He weaved his way towards us hiccuping loudly and slurring his words, then slipped in the mud, began to crawl in circles on all fours and vomited copiously and loudly, after which he began to choke and passed out cold: I could tell at once he had been drinking. With some reluctance I dried off, draped him over my handlebars and pedalled hard, depositing him in his college rooms where, as I had feared and just as I was tiptoeing away, he became emotional and began to unburden himself. To a man of my background and intellectual training these personal disclosures are particularly odious, not merely inappropriate but somehow jarring, like an African on a scholarship. Anyhow he told of a night in Soho when, flown with wine, he had gone to see a film to be ashamed of. On leaving the cinema he had stumbled, and was asked by a young man with fair hair was he all right who then commented as they emerged into the air on a change in the weather. Rigsby then followed him on impulse to the park where all sense was lost. He ended up walking back to his club sans wallet and bloodynosed. When he had finished he sat back sweating and of course began to blubber. I shook his hand, thanked him profusely then made my excuses and got out as quickly as I could. As I pedalled home

my mind was on fire. The colours of the sunset and the flowers in suburban gardens seemed more vivid than usual, and I thought back to the vial of colourless liquid I had absent-mindedly swallowed in the lab that day, mistaking it for a glass of water. My feet hardly seemed to touch the garden path and I felt illuminated by a quite extraordinary sensation of euphoria, coupled with a sense that the scales were falling from my eyes, indeed that I was growing new eyes, and scales, and that at any moment I might take wing. Humming I made my way into the kitchen and, rubbing my legs together with anticipation, sat down to eat a two-pound bag of sugar. But it was at that moment that I

became conscious of my wife silhouetted in the moonlight, wearing Capri pants under one of my old shirts, and smoking a St Moritz. As she turned her gaze towards me, eyes heavily underlined with kohl, I remembered that it was Friday night. Reaching behind my ear, I surreptitiously withdrew the zinc lozenge and slid it into the earth of an aspidistra that immediately spun on its roots, stared at me in disbelief, and withered. Bunny had never looked so alluring. We fell into an embrace, rolling over and over through shadow and moonlight on the kitchen floor as all our neighbours simultaneously took up the electric guitar and the 1950s sighed and sang goodbye. Our lovemaking was a long story with a happy ending, as we made our way from kitchen via lounge and landing to the master bedroom. That final time left us drifting into sleep on the far side of an aching sweetness that was almost pain, intense yet barely there. And this time I hadn't even needed Waltzes by Strauss to rev up the old Spitfire. We were just drifting off, cradled in each other's arms, when

a crash of glass disturbed the hush. It was our lodger, a young thug named Hughes reading Anthropology. He made his way unsteadily up the stairs cursing occasionally and muttering in his flat northern accent some gibberish about American women and legs that went on forever. I was in no mood for this. As he crossed the landing through a shaft of moonlight my years of training as a commando flooded back as if it were yesterday. I kicked his shin, whereupon with a look of surprise he fell through an open window and landed three floors down in the garden, moaning and bloodied. To my intense disgust he then sat up and began to thank me profusely. I had made him a poet by showing him the secret tryst of lyricism and physical catharsis. I tried to close my ears to this folly, which only grew in volume and idiocy. Nerves badly jangled I woke Anna, I mean Bunny, and we spent the remainder of the night huddled at the kitchen table, drinking tea in whispers. He was still raving about magical beasts and the zodiac after a disconcertingly massive explosion following a brilliant flash of light abruptly removed the house. He had thoroughly spoiled our evening.

31 MARJORIE WELISH

Detained By Rest

Detain nature in facsimile across nonchalance, against the grain. What is an
equivalent mat?

                Matter

translated and unlike, yet presumed in the phrase "our pro-foreignness"
or perhaps "aspirin". And "lyricism"

                as cars

into carp. With carp permitted and speaking of impossibility, "soluble
fish," neither described nor defined stay far from comprehending white,
black, assiduously translating all this into a house, coincidently your havoc.

Do we require an ambulance? An ambulance to give a close reading and apply
instrumentality? Do you require sleep, do you require little sleep? They
lack sleep yet do not need it. They like entering into sincerity little
by little, toward subsidence. Under your very eyes is a little less rest.
Inhabitants detained by rest do not find sleep now, now lost

in cheap images. And entities move ordinarily fatigued, with
metal fatigue against iron, cast fatigue and sleep transpiring
a sentence notwithstanding plainness. Then there is less
fence in question.

Nettles are natural
reproof, properly of allergy (Helen had been deployed already). And ahead
travelers merge with stairs' rate of change.
On a list of things,
vagrants are decoded by mood, are decided by vagaries. Visitors enter the
Visitors' Entrance, also known as the Staff Entrance. At the border,
something points to its object: Bear right and take the lift to the fifth floor.
Follow the sign, indicating the way to the elevator; take it to the fifth floor.
Go right to the lift and press "5" for staff offices. A lift for all occasions
is somewhere positive in this facility, this district, these uphill areas.

A change of
address: onto a fire escape in darkness, as a former architect,
for whom, like largesse over building, we are composing
translated fire escapes. The ones I have emphasized recant their

position, jet
West and East.

The politics of reading

have caught those moving stairs (as they were once called),
for epic purposes. In what sense are they then translations? In the climbing
valley,
our gradual ascent, our newly incremental elevation ready-to-hand,
escalators

are
"redirected toward unprohibited objects." (" Faster," say the montagists.)
Recite

something. Paraphrase a house or, in a phrase.

under deleterious influence, mentioning red, you pause at a district. I
forget the way back The implausibility of translation confronts
the necessity of translation, commissioning descriptions of doing so. I forgot
the way back from scale to size. This is my portion.
                    Off these rocks,

sincerity did escort authenticity once; once, sincerity did shoulder
mountains in snow. Then later. Literary torsos placed there cope with their
                                     being prior.
When you say "public" which public? When? Why? Or alternatively,

deputy literary critics translate business listings into beauty: heavily again,
her own criteria list
                lend
regularities
                stipulating this rock, these discursive rocks.

Macbeth in Battle

"Let's get married." "That's False."
"Not unmarried," she estimated.

Redness is whimsical or whitened. "I wonder
where my wallet is?" is not a question

but an implicit temptation trafficking
in interrogatives. Adam and Eve

encumbered.
                    Between languages

subsisting on value, and modernism.
The idea of gray is not a true copy.

                         "Don't!"

as a bridle for packages intimidated
amid prehensile pathways.

"What's the manner with you?"

                         "Ready, or not!"
if you rotate the letter 'N'

in your dialect of mathematics. And on a dark night,
bridle, strap, leash, vanilla, are celebratory.

Imagining vanilla, the reliable confection
luckily aestheticized, we are tempted to say,

chasing ethics
after surgery.

Using clues: it is raining, it is not raining. Do not eat knives frozen.
"Excuse me?"

Do not eat peas with a knife, knives.

"Excuse me?"

In brain areas,

"RAW" in neon
making "WAR"—
or else!
Physical interference

yet non-contradiction
mentions why.

Textile 9

"you refuse to become a deer or a tree"
     Pictorial. if contemporary—no contemporarily:
          We

a deer again
     Is contemporary art modern?
          She

as girl inhabited. inhabiting thirsty house, Louise—
     "an iconographic setback"
          You

This dark tree improvising
     pictorialism how many faces can you find?
          He

A form of because
     finding faces is explanatory, *malheureusement.*
          We

a form of because
     in surface

causing
     a white wall as an effect of modernity at midnight
          Plane

formulates because
     insofar as hunting, has brought a buck into meter, the
                    hunter's meter
          Reflective surface

insofar as
     the silhouetted tree is a semblance silhouetted tree, a
                    semblance
          of an aspect

of Goethe,
      Of Goethe arborescent, in an aspect of being afflicted
          surface

a surfeit of aspect, affect
      of Goethe as textual: more text than house, housed
          Point

as a net: they have netted themselves
      a form of because in pointing to it.
          Point to it.

Being chased.
      Directly to poetics.
          A slice.

Textile 11

Because. then
    if, then, then even as
        such as in voiceover

"'because,' Schubert writes . . ."
    "'Nevertheless, your life/ seems to me wide with potential
        [because of your/. . .'"

"because" pageant:
    to give voice to a cause
        choir

to ascertain causes beyond rhetoric
    chorus.

Causality in lyric is trying.
    A song, a song beyond rhetoric
        ours

insofar as . . .
    let us each in turn declare

causes
    the disenchantment to which we write cheques

"Nevertheless. your life/ seems to me wide with potential
    because of your/
        modesty."

        A vocal
"'because', Schubert writes"
    a voiceprint

"'as if'. Franz Schubert writes"
    I am here

"because" pageant in the twentieth century.
A path limited
mitered, yet a path

because, in the sense of
"That I am here"
Encore

or to give voice to a cause beyond rhetoric.
Let us each voice
(the vocals of . . .)

the causes to which we do in fact write cheques
(Tell 'em. Ella)

Textile 12

A path formatted. A chapter
  "There cannot be a chapter formatted differently,"

she said, "like a sore thumb."
  "A chapter formatted differently from these is not a sore thumb,"

I said, "But an opposable thumb, an opposable thumb with its
                                                own instrumentality."
  A train

"... hear that train strumming ... "
  "without the doubt of a shadow"

Agora shadowless and "shadowless"
  path.

Which?
  "In recent years he has researched the share"

a path formatted across a wave.
  There cannot be a wave formatted otherwise

she said, like a wheel.
  A wave in syntax such as that is no sore wheel.

I said but a solemn wheel (no one-sided wheel, I said, a level), with
  its own instrumentality. A door

"folded like a sheet of paper ... "
  "You were the most beautiful of them all."

"Now I begin to paint shadows in."
  Out-of-print—

which?

    In recent years he has researched the interval

which

    has researched the inconvenience

across hot water.

    There cannot be hot water formatted symptomatically,

she said, like fumes.

Textile 13

Locomotive

What is a portrait?
Locomotive

When is a portrait not a portrait?
When it is locomotive
not physiognomic

insofar as pasturing.
"Tendency of ideas to go over into movement"
Movement

as such.
Movement was used.
Walking along a walk

"As fully as possible."
Walking the walk.
Stance? Pavement?

As passage.
As passage to pavement
walking the walk

republished as
"Tendency of ideas to go over into movement.
For these experiments

the subject was given a pencil."
By the people.
Men At Work.

As in the phrase
"working women."

32 JOHN WILKINSON

Sideshow

What shall divide me now?
Unpick the seam
                  the wound
whose guts went out,
      conquering space.
My wound has been crowded
full as a corpse of self

Beside me the hum continues
      breaking into song—
no, hardly amiss within
day's labour & the body's
      exactions—
         this is not cleaned up
or wrapped or binned,

but sustains its note
      alongside, & keeps time
for alibi that its droning suits.
        Tight neck
lets balloon or shrivels
marks or in qualities,
dominant all the same

as thinking carries forward
      down its forks
by Type & by Creator.
For they have both to be

plied, & the knife
            too as needs must;
& these were the pent cutlery
thought's song works with,
worrying a tip
            under the matted-
down stitch, easing
the categorical thread.
                    Unhook
its prosodion I, no longer taut.

Oiled Sweater

Though splinted a controlling thumb
      has its uses, at remove
unmans what threw the shiny ball,
        but quivering on the trampoline
           yanks the facings do not yield
like drips & webs of fat though wanted.
Taut stays that had once burnt
      burn & burn again
           Twist this cap off & up

might say almost comforted.
The locks of rope usefully could ward
the spiced already
      charms of such a harbour,
      sinking thought into
chosen words.
    Let them intercalate their pins
      their acronymic files
   the tumblers that jar so firm
O thumb your nose at these, at least

recollect in the trampoline,
               gently
having been primed to rebuff
    like a resolvent
        trembles like
the avoided sea
        does against the eye,
rigged against a rough white backdrop
bounces the distressed bladder
springs the weakening voice.
    Balls fly out behind laurels
        out of the boathouse,
all going uncaught. They must suffice.

Grace

Light so intensifies the ghost holds off
as a sign of a more dubitable way
If you wore a veil I might touch

the swaddled core, be burnt & thrilled
But over distance, sun & cloud
play advocate, remote & simultaneous.

This translation from your far booth
makes for a presence which is so
tenuous but snapping at the tip of

ubiquitin, don't get cut off in dispersal
chain-drive having been seen to fetch,
though obscure trees & ornaments

structuring but dead without this flicker
retrace that I clutch it undischarged.

The Torn Ones

The scenery bows for you & the skies defer.
However stressed-out you are,
the connections will be reliable, the service
not interrupted. Shower-gel & powder
now carry the brand world-wide,
finance that regime will keep you in shape.
The fat of the land flies to be eaten to be
worked off. What stays back has definition
according to the best lens. Bring
a glass of chablis from the fridge,
slate investigation for an ulcer to be wiped.
No.7 handle with the Zurich edge I think.

I think the best they have is an old tooth
of yours & it does not bring money or even
seed in the morning voiding its void,
but rips out gifts which require
every defined stick, every jewel-like drop
& are implacably loved in the sun splendent.

The Rest of It

Secret pillagers that protect the heart
unwittingly open like a mould
the never courteous
mirror floor.
What now floats decays & is knowing
drives the primrose nail into
amputated earth
will not rise
gaily to hobble. Fronds inter
leave & the occupier pulls his weight
in froth & froth lives.

Pink sang-froid, sky over
wretched wounds in the victory pillar.

The Impatient Man Kills with his Piano-playing

Aluminium shed the grab-hook
    finds light & lifts,
a hand that claws
    about the keyboard, scattering
    matt grains of metal.
Gift the ochre,
    gift the empty amber, the
pillowcases void of feathers,
    lost steps. Such plenitude
in more of less, quilted in its blank looks.

To say 'Go hang' goes hang,
    its efficacy
derives from not-quite, from this-short.
    Rub the amber, tinkle
    at the ivories—
but a tusk breaks through the sound-board
singing but too amply.
Is there a riff
behind the broken arpeggio, an engine
    behind the disciplined snarl,
saying I am he who . . . ?

Other voices hang in green pips.
    Not the recapitulation
smacks the ear or tooth or nettled jaw—
    if the subject
    is already multiple,
one is produced by its desire O surely
not. Each is enviable
    gashes through a silk
presentation case—but the ring
passes officiously to the shortlist finger.

Hammer away at its privileges
      as on a glockenspiel,
      a sprite on the many anvils.
         Faculae
are the stub theory will estimate each star,
the lit quartz rods programming a face.

      They will excite a voice,
promote the economy of a honeycomb,
quilted like sand when the ebb is lowest,
quilted like irregular fields
      regularly dash the eye.

Funk Qualms

Stuffed like a scarecrow, are these
genuine boundaries I asked as between
tillers of earth, or signals I hope not.

If there is no bone it is a breast, if
no nipple it is an open pit I am clawing.
A decompressor was candied in blood.

Yes I want to have this so I can swap
for something ephemeral I can now miss
that badly it will be mine for always.

Notes on the Contributors

John Ashbery

John Ashbery was awarded the Pulitzer Prize, the National Book Critics Circle Award and the National Book Award for *Self-Portrait in a Convex Mirror* (1975), and since that time has been celebrated in America and abroad. He has been named a Guggenheim and a MacArthur Fellow, and served as Chancellor of the Academy of American Poets from 1988–99. He was Charles Eliot Norton Professor of Poetry at Harvard. Since 1990 he has been Charles P. Stevenson, Jnr Professor of Languages and Literature at Bard College in Annandale-on-Hudson, New York. His work has been translated into more than twenty languages. He has published over twenty books of poetry, most recently *Your Name Here* (Farrar, Straus and Giroux, 2000) and *As Umbrellas Follow Rain* (Qua Books, 2001) and *Chinese Whispers* (Farrar, Straus and Giroux, 2002). Almost all of John Ashbery's books are available from Carcanet in the United Kingdom.

Caroline Bergvall

Caroline Bergvall is a poet and text-based artist based in London, England. Her books include *Eclat* (Sound&Language, 1996), *Goan Atom, 1: Doll* (Krupskaya, 2001). Widely featured in magazines in the US and Europe, a selection of her work has appeared in the *Oxford Anthology of Modern British and Irish Poetry*, ed. Keith Tuma (OUP, 2001). She has developed audiotexts as well as collaborative performances and installations with artists in galleries and at festivals. Most recently, the sound-text installation *Say: "Parsley"* at the Liverpool Biennial (2004). Other recent outputs include: *GONG* (Belladonna, NY: 2004) and *8 Figs* (Equipage, Cambridge: 2004), *Eclat* redesigned as a pdf book for ubuweb. Her collection *FIG (Goan Atom, 2)* is due out with Salt in 2005.

Her critical work is chiefly concerned with context-led writing and performance text practices. She was Director of Performance Writing at Dartington College of Arts (1995–2000). She is currently Associate Research Fellow in Performance Writing at Dartington and is on the Writing faculty of the MFA at Bard College (NY).

Lee Ann Brown

Lee Ann Brown's first full-length collection of poetry, *Polyverse* (Sun & Moon Press, 1999) won the New American Poetry Prize and her second book, *The Sleep that Changed Everything* is being published by Wesleyan University Press in 2003. She was born in Saitama-ken, Japan and raised in Charlotte, North Carolina. Ms Brown earned her BA at Brown University in 1987, then moved to New York City where she founded Tender Buttons press which publishes innovative writing by women. She worked at the Poetry Project at St Mark's Church from 1988 until 1991 and then returned to Brown for an MFA (1993). Since then, she has taught at several universities in the United States and is currently Assistant Professor of English at St John's University. Her honours and awards have included fellowships from the New York Foundation for the Arts, the Fund for Poetry, and the Fondation Royaumont, as well as fellowships from the MacDowell Colony, Djerassi Artists Residency, the Rocky Mountain Women's Institute, Yaddo and the Virginia Center for the Creative Arts. Ms Brown's poetry has been published in numerous journals and periodicals and was recently included in *The Best American Poetry* 2001 edited by Robert Hass. Lee Ann Brown performs her work internationally and works in film, video and song in addition to being a poet.

Brian Catling

Brian Catling was born in London in 1948. His publications include *The Stumbling Block: its Index* (Bookworks, 1990), *Soundings: a Tractate of Absence* (Matt's Gallery, 1991), *The Blindings* (Bookworks, 1995), *Late Harping: Last Century Works* (Etruscan Books, 2001), *Large Ghost* (Equipage, 2001) and *Thyhand* (Alfred David Editions, 2001). He is a sculptor and performance artist whose most recent solo shows have been at the Project Gallery, Leipzig, Matt's Gallery, London, the ICA,

London and Galleri s.e. Bergen. He is Professor of Fine Art at the University of Oxford and Head of Sculpture and Graduate Studies at the Ruskin School of Drawing. He is a fellow of Linacre College, Oxford.

DAVID CHALONER

David Chaloner was born in Cheshire in 1944 and lives in London. *Delight's Wreckage* was published by Shearsman/Oasis in the summer of 2001, the first full length collection since *Trans* (Galloping Dog Press, 1989). *Art for Others* (1998) and *The Edge* (1993) were both published in the Equipage series and *Where Once Was* and *Villa of Mysteries* appeared from Poetical Histories in 1989 and 2001. A selection of work appeared in the anthology *A State of Independence* from Stride Publications, edited by Tony Frazer.

ANDREW CROZIER

"Nobody is the author of his own life story." Crozier continues to have been born in 1943. Trauma of entering the world in rural Hertfordshire as one of blitzed London's evacuees may explain some resistance to displacement and for the time being he has lived and worked in East Sussex since 1973. An edition of his collected poems, *All Where Each Is*, was published in 1985, and is available on the Chadwyck-Healy *Twentieth Century English Poetry* full-text database, as is his later *Free Running Bitch*.

ANDREW DUNCAN

Andrew Duncan grew up in Loughborough but lives in North London. He is the author of various books of poetry (*Cut Memories and False Commands, Alien Skies, Sound Surface, Anxiety before entering a room, Switching and Main Exchange, Skeleton Looking at Chinese Pictures, Pauper Estate*, etc.) and is well known as an editor, particularly of *Angel Exhaust*. He is currently working on two books, *Symbolic Machines* and *Savage Survivals*.

Roy Fisher

Roy Fisher was born in Birmingham in 1930 and taught in the Department of American Studies at Keele University. He now lives in the Peak District of Derbyshire. He wrote *The Cut Pages* in 1970 and it was first published in the year following by Fulcrum Press.

Lionel Fogarty

Born in Queensland in Australia in 1958, Lionel Fogarty is a leading representative of aboriginal literature. Lionel Fogarty grew up on a reservation, at the age of 18 he ran away to Brisbane, where he joined various self-help organisations of Aborigines for whom he wrote articles and gave speeches. Lionel Fogarty has published five poetry volumes and a collection of poems and tales called *Munaldjali, Mutuerjaraea*. In them he objects to having his language (Murri) drawn into English, so draws English into his own aboriginal space-time continuum. His collected poems, *Dha'lan Djani Mitti* is forthcoming from Salt.

Ulli Freer

Ulli Freer lives in London. His recent publications include *Blvd.s* (Equipage, 1994) and *eye line* (Spanner, 1996). His work has also been published in several anthologies, including *Other: British and Irish Poetry since* 1970 (Wesleyan University Press, 1999).

Peter Gizzi

Peter Gizzi was born in 1959 and grew up in New England. His poetry publications include *Some Values of Landscape and Weather* (Wesleyan University Press, 2003), *Artificial Heart* (Burning Deck, 1998), and *Periplum and other poems* (1987–1992) (Salt Publishing, 2004), among others. He has been awarded artist grants from The Fund for Poetry (1993), Rex Foundation (1994), the Howard Foundation (1998), and The Foundation for Contemporary Performance Arts (1999). In 1994 he received the prestigious Lavan Younger Poets Award from the Academy of American Poets. His editing projects have included the celebrated "little magazine" *o.blek: a journal of language arts* (1987–93), the international literary anthology the *Exact Change Yearbook* (Carcanet, 1995), and *The House that Jack Built: The Collected Lectures of Jack Spicer* (Wesleyan University Press, 1998).

LISA JARNOT

Lisa Jarnot is the author of *Phonetic Introductions* (Northern Lights, 1988), *The Fall of Orpheus* (Shuffaloff Press, 1993), *Some Other Kind of Mission* (burning Deck Press, 1996), *Sea Lyrics* (Situations Press, 1996) and *Heliopolis* (rem press, 1998). Her most recent collection of poems, *Ring of Fire*, is forthcoming from Zoland Books. She was a co-editor of *An Anthology of (American) Poets* from Talisman House Publishers in 1997, and from 1996 through 1998 was the editor of the *Poetry Project Newsletter* in New York City. She currently lives in Brooklyn, New York where she is an Assistant Professor at Long Island University and where she is writing a biography of the American poet Robert Duncan.

MICHELE LEGGOTT

Michele Leggott (b. 1956) is an Associate Professor in English at the University of Auckland and founding coordinator in 2001 of the New Zealand Electronic Poetry Centre (nzepc). Poetry collections include *Like This?* (1988), *Swimmers, Dancers* (1991), *DIA* (1994) and *As far as I can see* (1999); *milk and honey* is due from Auckland UP and Salt Publishing in 2005. Critical and editorial work includes *Reading Zukofsky's "80 Flowers"* (Johns Hopkins UP, 1989), *Big Smoke: New Zealand Poems 1960–1975*, with co-editors Alan Brunton and Murray Edmond (Auckland UP, 2000) and *Young Knowledge: The Poems of Robin Hyde* (Auckland UP, 2003). See also nzepc author page at www.nzepc.auckland.ac.nz/authors/leggott/

TONY LOPEZ

Tony Lopez lives in Devon and works for the University of Plymouth where he is the first Professor of Poetry. He has received awards from The Society of Authors (1990) and from The Wingate Foundation (1996). Since the publication of his first American book by The Figures in 1996 he has travelled widely on reading tours all over USA and Canada. His most recent poetry books are *Devolution* (The Figures, 2000), *Data Shadow* (Reality Street, 2000) and *False Memory* (Salt, 2003). Anthology appearances include *Twentieth-Century British and Irish Poetry* (OUP, 2001), *Other: British and Irish Poetry since 1970* (Wesleyan University Press, 1999) and *Conductors of Chaos* (Picador, 1996). Further information is available at www.soton.ac.uk/~bepc/poets/lopez_1.htm

BARRY MACSWEENEY

Barry MacSweeney was born in Newcastle-upon-Tyne in 1948. At sixteen he left school to work on various provincial newspapers as an investigative reporter, industrial correspondent and news editor. His publications include *The Boy From the Green Cabaret Tells of His Mother* (Hutchinson, 1968), *Our Mutual Scarlet Boulevard* (Fulcrum 1971), *Brother Wolf* (Turret, 1972), *Odes* (Trigram, 1978), *Ranter* (Slow Dancer, 1985), *Hellhound Memos* (The Many Press, 1993), *Pearl* (Equipage, 1985), *The Book of Demons* (Bloodaxe, 1997), *Sweet Advocate* (Equipage, 1999), *Wolf Tongue: Selected Poems 1965–2000* (Bloodaxe, 2003). His last book was *Horses in Boiling Blood* (Equipage, 2004). MacSweeney died in 2000.

ANNA MENDELSSOHN

Anna Mendelssohn was born in Cheshire in 1948. She trained through the New Era Academy of Drama and Music (1957–67) and performed in Northern Music Festivals until 1967. She was educated at Stockport High School for Girls, and at the University of Essex (1967–9). She spent the following year in Turkey, teaching English and French and translating 1930s Turkish poetry, surrealist and social realist. She has lived in Stockport, London, Sheffield and Cambridge. As Grace Lake she has published *Viola Tricolor* (1993), *Bernache Nonette* (1995) and *Tondo Aquatique* (1997), all with Equipage, and as Anna Mendelssohn she has published *Implacable Art* (2000) with Folio/Equipage.

DREW MILNE

Drew Milne was born in Edinburgh in 1964 and currently works as the Judith E.Wilson Lecturer in Drama and Poetry, University of

Cambridge. His books of poetry include *Satyrs and Mephitic Angels* (1993), *Sheet Mettle* (1994), *Songbook* (1996), *Bench Marks* (1998), *As It Were* (1998), *Pianola* (1999), *familiars* (1999), *The Gates of Gaza* (2000), *The Damage: new and selected poems* (Salt, 2001) and *Mars Disarmed* (The Figures, 2002). He has also edited the journal *Parataxis: modernism and modern writing.*

JENNIFER MOXLEY

Jennifer Moxley is the author of *Imagination Verses* (Tender Buttons 1996; Salt 2003), *The Sense Record and other poems* (Edge 2002; Salt 2003) and *Often Capital* (Flood 2005). Her translation of the French poet Jacqueline Risset's 1976 book *The Translation Begins* was published by Burning Deck in 1996. She lives in Orono, Maine and works as an Assistant Professor of Creative Writing at the University of Maine.

IAN PATTERSON

Ian Patterson teaches English at Queens' College, Cambridge. His translation of Proust's *Le Temps retrouve* is published by Viking Penguin in 2002. In the 1990s he published *Roughly Speaking* and *Tense Fodder,* and featured in the anthology *Conductors of Chaos* (edited by Iain Sinclair, Picador, 1996). His most recent book is *Much More Pronounced* (Equipage, 1999). The full sequence of 'Hardihood' will be published in *Hardihood and other poems.*

J.H. PRYNNE

J.H. Prynne was born in Kent and studied at Cambridge, where he currently works. He has published some twenty-seven collections of poems during the period 1968–2003. which plus one further sequence previously unpublished will be included in the reissued and expanded *Poems* shortly to appear (2005) from Fremantle Arts Centre Press and Bloodaxe Books. Four recent collections (including the full text of *Red D Gypsum*) have in addition been republished in America under the interim title *Furtherance* (The Figures, 2004). There is also a separately published commentary on Shakespeare's *Sonnets*, 94 (2001). His travels have included many visits to foreign parts variously far-flung; his work has been translated into several foreign languages, notably French and German but also Italian, Danish and Chinese.

Peter Riley

Born 1940, Stockport, near Manchester, in an environment of working people, and entered higher education through Britain's post-war socialistic educational policies. Read English at Cambridge and has since lived and worked in London, Hastings, Hove, Odense (Denmark), and the Peak District, in various kinds of teaching and casual employment. Since 1985 he has lived in Cambridge, where he operates the last surviving mail-order poetry book business. He has written studies of Jack Spicer, T.F. Powys, improvised music, poetry, lead mines, burial mounds and Transylvanian string bands. His poetry has appeared in ten principal collections: *Love-Strife Machine* (1968); *The Linear Journal* (1973); *Lines on the Liver* (1981); *Tracks and Mineshafts* (1983); *Sea Watches* (1991); *Distant Points (Excavations Part One Books One and Two)* (1995); *Noon Province* (1996); *Snow Has Settled...Bury Me Here* (1997); *Passing Measures* a selected poems, (Carcanet, 2000); *The Dance at Mociu* (prose: sketches of Transylvania) Shearsman 2003; *Aria with Small Lights* (West House Books, 2003); *Alstonefield: a poem* (Carcanet, 2003); *Excavations* complete edition (Reality Street, 2004); *A Map of Faring* (Parlor Press, USA, forthcoming 2004). He has translated the French poet Lorand Gaspar *(Four Poems*, 1993) who has, with others, reciprocally translated a bilingual selection (*Noon Province et autres poemes*, 1996).

Lisa Robertson

Born in Toronto, Canadian writer Lisa Robertson lived in Vancouver for twenty-three years, where she was a treeplanter, a cook, a bookseller, an editor, a teacher, and a participant in the continuing utopian experiment called The Kootenay School of Writing. She has recently moved to Paris. Her books of poetry include *XEclogue, Debbie: An Epic, The Weather* (New Star Books/ Reality Street Editions) and *Rousseau's Boat* (Nomados). Newly published by Clear Cut Press is *Occasional Works and Seven Walks from the Office for Soft Architecture*, a linked series of prose essays on cities, architecture and ornament.

STEPHEN RODEFER

The American writer Stephen Rodefer, whose books include *Four Lectures*, *VILLON* by Jean Calais, *Mon Canard* and *Left Under a Cloud*, among many others, has taught at the University of California, New York University, the University of Cambridge, and at the American University in Paris, where he now lives. His collected essays *The Monkey's Donut* will be published by Kollophon in 2005.

GIG RYAN

Gig Ryan, born in 1956, lived in Sydney from 1978 to 1990, when she returned to Melbourne. In 1993, she took a B.A. in Classics at the University of Melbourne. Her books include *The Division of Anger* (Transit Press, 1981), *Manners of an Astronaut* (Hale & Iremonger, 1984), *The Last Interior* (Scripsi Publications, 1986), *Excavation* (PanPicador Australia, 1990), *Research* (excerpt from *Pure and Applied*) (Folio/Salt, 1998), *Pure and Applied* (Paper Bark Press/ Craftsman House, 1998), *Heroic Money* (Brandl & Schlesinger, 2001). As a musician, she has put out *Six Goodbyes* (songs with Disban, Big Home Recordings, 1988) and *Real Estate* (songs with Driving Past, Chapter Music, 1999). A new CD with Driving Past is forthcoming.

JOHN TRANTER

'*from* Blackout' is an excerpt from the chapbook *Blackout*, first published by Barque Press, Cambridge UK, 2000, also published by Vagabond Press, Sydney, in 2000. *Blackout* consists of Shakespeare's *The Tempest*, the article 'Some Dreamers of the Golden Dream' by Joan Didion, and a chapter from *The Electric Kool-Aid Acid Test* by Tom Wolfe, with most of the words removed, and the remaining words and phrases interleaved, though in the same order as they appear in the original texts. No other words have been added.

John Tranter has published twenty collections of verse, including *Heart Print*, *Studio Moon* and *Trio* (all published by Salt in the U.K.) In 1992 he edited (with Philip Mead) the *Penguin Book of Modern Australian Poetry*, which has become the standard text in its field. He has lived at various times in Melbourne (Australia), London, Singapore, Brisbane (Australia), Florida and San Francisco, and now lives in Sydney, where he is a company director. He is the editor of the free Internet magazine *Jacket*, at http://jacketmagazine.com/

GEOFF WARD

Geoff Ward was born in 1954. He has published six collections of poems, including a barbarous recasting of Rilke's *Duino Elegies* (Equipage, 1998). His public readings have included performances at the Cambridge Conference of Contemporary Poetry; Segue Foundation, New York; and Tokyo Metropolitan University. Professor of English at the University of Dundee, he has published several critical works including *The Writing of America* (Polity, 2002). He has held a Leverhulme Fellowship (1999-2001) and in 2001 he was named a Fellow of the Royal Society of the Arts.

MARJORIE WELISH

Marjorie Welish is a poet and critic living in New York. Her poetry books include: *Casting Sequences* (University of Georgia Press, 1993), *Else, in Substance* (Paradigm Press, 1999), *The Annotated "Here" and Selected Poems* (Coffee House Press, 2000) and *Begetting Textile* (Equipage, 2000), this last written in partial fulfilment of a Howard Foundation Fellowship from Brown University. Her criticism may be found in *Signifying Art: Essays on Art after 1960* (Cambridge University Press, 1999) and in the *Encyclopaedia of Aesthetics* (Oxford University Press, 1998) and elsewhere.

JOHN WILKINSON

John Wilkinson was born in London in 1953 and grew up in Cornwall and Devon. Having spent his working life in mental health, latterly as a strategic planner in the east end of London, in 2005 he was appointed Poet in Resident at the Keough Institute for Irish Studies, University of Notre Dame. His numerous pamphlets of poetry have been collected in *Clinical Notes* (1980), *Proud Flesh* (1986), *Flung Clear* (1994), *Oort's Cloud* (1999) and *Effigies Against the Light* (2001). Most recently he has published the volume *Contrivances* (2003) and the pamphlet *Iphigenia* (2004).

ACKNOWLEDGMENTS

John Ashbery: "All Messages Have Been Played," published in *Van Gogh's Ear* (Paris). "A Holding Mode," published as "Because the Night," in *Mudfish* (New York). "Franchises in Flux," first published in *Aphros* (New York). "Nut Castle" published as "Immoral Streams," in *Bard Papers*. "Interesting People of Newfoundland," "Meaningful Love," published in *PN Review*. "Wolf Ridge," published in *Conjunctions*. "The Template" published in the *Times Literary Supplement*. All poems copyright © 2003 John Ashbery. Reprinted by permission of the author.

Caroline Bergvall: "Hungry Form," copyright © 1994 Caroline Bergvall. From *Milk of Late*, Cambridge: Equipage, 1994. Reprinted by permission of the author and the publisher.

Lee Ann Brown: "My epithalamion," first published in *An Anthology of New (American) Poets*, edited by Lisa Jarnot, Chris Stroffolino and Leonard Schwartz, Talisman House (1998). "You Are Not Gorgeous and I Am Coming Anyway," first published in *Snare*, Issue 2, New York City, edited by Drew Gardner, Fall 2000. "My Uncruel April, My Totally Equal Unforetold April Unfolded," "The Impulse to Call & Spring Upon," was first published in *The Voluptuary Lion Poems of Spring* (Tender Buttons, 1997). "Respond to me," appeared in a pamphlet, *Miss Traduction*, Centre de Poésie et Traduction & Tender Lynx, Fondation Royaumont, France, 1995. "shiny jewel eye," was first published in The Portable Boog Reader, edited by David Kirschenbaum, Boog Literature, New York City, 2000. "A Call for Vertical Integration in the Eye of the Storm," first published in *Jacket*, edited by John Tranter, Volume 8, http://jacketmagazine.com/08/index.html. "Encyclopedia Botanica," copyright © Lee Ann Brown.

Brian Catling: "The Pittancer," copyright © Brian Catling. Reprinted by permission of the author.

David Chaloner: "Waste," "Unnamed," "Emblem," "Spring and Other Places," "Thicket of Time," "Vista Vert," copyright © David Chaloner. Reprinted by permission of the author.

Andrew Crozier: "Humiliation in its Disguises," © Andrew Crozier, 1985. "Blank Misgivings," first published in *Gard du Nord*, Volume 1, No. 3, 1998, edited by Alice Notley and Douglas Oliver. Reprinted by permission of the author.

Andrew Duncan: "Andy-the-German Servant of Two Masters," "The Ghost of Fusion," "The Shield of Perseus," "Martyrdom and Triumph of Sergei Korolev," copyright © Andrew Duncan. Reprinted by permission of the author.

Roy Fisher: from "The Cut Pages," copyright © Roy Fisher. From *The Cut Pages*, London: Fulcrum Press, 1971. Reprinted by permission of the author.

Lionel Fogarty: "By Accident, Blinked," "Am I," "Memo to Us (story)," "Kath Walker," "Fuck All Departments," "Biral Biral," copyright © Lionel G. Fogarty. From *New and Selected Poems: Munaldjali, Mutuerjaraera*, Melbourne: Hyland House, 1999. Reprinted by permission of the author.

Ulli Freer: "fragmento," copyright © Ulli Freer. A version of "fragmento" was first published in *Jacket* issue 10, 2000. From *Speakbright Leap Passwood: New and Selected Poems*, Cambridge: Salt Publishing, 2003. Reprinted by permission of the author and the publisher.

Peter Gizzi: "Lonely Tylenol," "Another Day on the Pilgrimage," "Fables of Critique," "Last Cigar," "Tous les Matins du Monde," "Ding Repair," all from *Artificial Heart* (Burning Deck, 1998).

Lyn Hejinian: "The Beginner," copyright © Lyn Hejinian. From *The Beginner*, Brooklyn: Spectacular Books. 2001. Reprinted by permission of the author.

Susan Howe, 2003; published in New Directions' 2003 edition of *The Midnight* and reprinted by permission of the author and New Directions Publishing Corporation: all rights reserved.

Lisa Jarnot: "Brooklyn Anchorage," "What In Fire Did I, Firelover, Starter of Fires, Love?," "The Specific Incendiaries of Springtime," "Still Life," "Valley of the Shadow of the Dogs," "Poem Beginning with a Line by Frank Lima," copyright © Lisa Jarnot. From *Ring of Fire*, Hanover: Zoland Books, 2001, reprinted by Cambridge: Salt Publishing 2003. Reprinted by permission of the author and the publishers.

John Kinsella: "Bluff Knoll Sublimity," "Akbar," "The Rust Eclogues: Radnoti, Poetry, and the Strains of Appropriation," "Radnoti Quarantine: Razglednicas," copyright © John Kinsella. From *The Radnoti Poems*, Cambridge: Equipage, 1996, reprinted in *Doppler Effect*, Salt Publishing 2004. Reprinted by permission of the author and the publisher.

Michele Leggott: "thoroughfares await them," "dark torch," "the songs of good hope," "omphalos," copyright © Michele Leggott. Reprinted by permission of the author.

Tony Lopez: 'In Memory' and 'Dint' from *Devolution* (2000) published by The Figures, copyright © Tony Lopez 2000; 'Studies in Classic American Literature' from *False Memory* (2003) published by Salt, copyright © Tony Lopez 2003.

Barry MacSweeney: "I Looked Down on a Child Today," was first published in *Tears in the Fence*, and was reprinted with "Totem Banking" in *Wolf Tongue: Selected Poems 1965–2000*, Newcastle: Bloodaxe, 2003. Reprinted with the permission of Bloodaxe Books Ltd. "Wreckage is the only Answer," "Seared to the echo," "Cute Petite," copyright © Barry MacSweeney. Thanks to the family of Barry MacSweeney, reprinted by permission of the Estate of Barry MacSweeney.

Anna Mendelssohn: "The wrong room," "Strictly personal," "Britain 1967," "On being reproached by saintly mediators for bad budgeting," "Franked," "Photrum," "footsteps climb whereas they descend," copyright © Anna Mendelssohn, 2004. Unpublished. Printed by permission of the author.

Rod Mengham: "Names in the Bark," "To the Soviet Embalmers," "Smitten," "Another Name for the Cassiterides," "Allegory of Good Government," "Concession to Perpetuity No. 166," copyright © Rod Mengham. From *Unsung: New and Selected Poems*, Cambridge: Salt Publishing, 2001. Reprinted by permission of the author and the publisher.

Drew Milne: from "Bench Marks," from "As It Were," copyright © Drew Milne. *The*

Printed in the United States
26550LVS00003B/302

9 781876 857134